BUBBE MEISES

(Yiddish idiom for Old Wives Tales)

BUBBE MEISES

Jewish Myths, Jewish Realities

Rabbi Ronald H. Isaacs

KTAV PUBLISHING HOUSE, INC.
Jersey City, New Jersey
2008

Library of Congress Cataloging-in-Publication Data

Isaacs, Ronald H.
Bubbe meises : Jewish myths, Jewish reality / Ronald H. Isaacs.
    p.   cm.
  ISBN 978-1-60280-032-8
  1. Judaism—Doctrines—Miscellanea.   2. Judaism—Customs
and practices—Miscellanea.   I. Title.
BM602.I73   2008
296 [22]   2008008766

Published by
KTAV Publishing House, Inc.
930 Newark Avenue
Jersey City, NJ 07306
Email: bernie@ktav.com
www.ktav.com
(201) 963-9524
Fax (201) 963-0102

Contents

Chapter Five
DEATH AND DYING

Chapter Six
RITUAL OBJECTS AND OBSERVANCES

Chapter Seven
JEWISH SUPERSTITIONS

Chapter 8
SEX

Chapter 11
MEDICAL ETHICS

Chapter 12
PRAYER

Chapter 13
BIBLE

Introduction

My grandparents are no longer alive, but I still cherish their many stories and good advice. My maternal grandmother, known in my household as bubbe Sadie, liked to remind me that I was her favorite grandchild (grandparents always seem to have a favorite). Born in Austria, she married at age sixteen and spoke a fluent Yiddish. She brought with her many local customs, expressions, language, superstitions, and **bubbe meises**, including the act of picking up one's ear. Picking up one's ear, of course, was a bubbe meise—to quote Leo Rosen, "an old wives' tale, something silly and untrue." And while maybe not true, it certainly at the time seemed silly. Still, it was a litany and a custom in my grandma's home.

I spent the first ten years of my life living with my parents in my bubbe Sadie's home, and throughout those years I heard her tell many stories and got lots of advice from her. Bubbe Sadie always told me that it was not a good idea to step on a crack while walking along a sidewalk, or for that matter to step on any threshold. When I asked her why, she simply said that it was bad luck to do so (A book on Jewish superstitions that I recently read stated that this superstition was based on the belief that demons, imps, elflocks, and the like lived under and inhabited thresholds and the general area of the door.). She also always reminded me to keep a pin on me at all times, but never explained why. (To this day I never throw away the pins that are attached to my dry-cleaned trousers. I have a whole box of them in my closet!) And the most incredible story she ever told me had to do with a piece of a red-and-green dress that her rebbe's wife, the rebbetzin, always enjoyed wearing. When the rebbetzin died, my bubbe asked whether she could have her dress. With no questions asked, the rebbe complied and my bubbe would often sleep with it adorning her pillow. As the dress began to fray and tear from use, my bubbe gave a piece of it to each of her thirty-six grandchildren. I still cherish my piece, and would never think of leaving it at home when confronting an important occasion. (It stayed in my pocket all through my defense of my doctoral dissertation! I got my doctorate, so it must have worked!)

I often fantasize what it would be like if she were here (she would be 107). Perhaps we would go to the movies together (she enjoyed westerns), and I surely would want her to meet her great-granddaughter Mimi (my first grandchild).

There's a Jewish tradition that when we are standing under the wedding canopy to get married, all of our deceased grandparents come and stand with us. I cannot imagine how improved everyday life would be if I could have real access to all those years of recipes, food delicacies, and especially hearing those bubbe meises. They've become a fabric of my life, and continue to warn me of things to do or not to do, activities in which to get involved and other things to avoid. As silly as some of these bubbe meises seem, I now realize that they were done with one sole concern. My bubbe wanted to keep me safe and protected in life.

Considering the long history of the Jewish people, it is not surprising that so many myths, misunderstandings, and bubba meises about Judaism have circulated and have been passed down from generation to generation. The process has continued to this day. With a career in the rabbinate now for almost a three and a half decades, I am intrigued by the many bubbe meises to which the Jewish people continue to cling. This volume is intended to present by topic some of my favorite myths and bubba meises associated with Judaism and Jewish living and then set the record straight. I hope to clarify and explain how many of these bubbe meises arose and why people continue not only to believe in them but to transmit them to their families. The writer Sasha Frieze once said that "bubbe meises aren't really old wives' tales. They're the cloth you're wrapped in at birth, and the fabric of your shroud when you die." I heartily agree with her. A good bubbe meise will stay with you for the rest of your life.

CHAPTER 1

Basic Jewish Beliefs

1. Judaism has no established creed for all Jews to follow

A dogma is usually defined as a doctrine of belief that has the support of a central authority such as the hierarchy of a church. It is generally agreed that the Hebrew Bible does not contain dogmas, nor does the Talmud (the rabbinic interpretation of the Bible) dwell on formulating them. Although most of us would like to be able to state what we believe, as well as to articulate the basic principles of Judaism in a few sentences, especially if we are asked questions about our religious beliefs and the Jewish tradition by others, it simply isn't that easy. Statements about Judaism for Jews to memorize and then repeat word for word to others would rob us of the opportunity to struggle with Jewish belief and arrive at a decision about personal faith on our own. Churches, however, do have dogmas for their adherents to follow. In Roman Catholicism, belief in the Trinity is an accepted dogma.

The Jewish people have never had a central authority that issued dogmas to which all Jews were required to adhere. Over the centuries Jewish scholars have asserted that Judaism contains no single creed, thus differentiating it from Christianity. The German philosopher Moses Mendelssohn posited that Judaism was primarily a rational religion, and that reason and dogma were incompatible. Judaism, he asserted, would never require Jews to accept a doctrine merely on faith, especially if such a doctrine was irrational.

Solomon Schechter, the Jewish Theological Seminary's first president, was the first to challenge Mendelssohn's view, in his essay "The Dogmas of Judaism." Although Schechter agreed that Judaism has no single authority that proclaims

Jewish dogma for all to follow, he contended that Judaism does contain doctrines of faith and guiding principles by which Jews are expected to lead their lives.

In the Mishnah Sanhedrin we find the beginning of a creed for Jews to follow: "These are excluded from the world-to-come: one who says there is no resurrection after death, one who denies that the Torah is divine, and the *epikoros*," often understood as one who denies belief in reward and punishment or who treats Scripture in a non-serious manner.

During the Middle Ages, when Judaism was being challenged by Greek philosophy, Islam, and Christianity, more serious attempts were made to establish a creed of dogma for all Jews to follow. The best-known of them was Moses Maimonides' Thirteen Principles of Faith, found in his commentary to the Mishnah (Sanhedrin 10:1). His creed included the principles of belief in the existence of an incorporeal and eternal God, belief in prophecy, belief that the Torah can never be changed, and belief in the coming of the Messiah. Maimonides went so far as to assert that Jews could not attain immortality if they did not adhere to certain specific beliefs. And he said that unbelievers were to be excluded from the Jewish community.

Maimonides' Thirteen Principles were accepted by many Jews and eventually made their way, with some variations, into many traditional prayerbooks. Each article of faith was introduced by the Hebrew words *ani ma'amin* ("I believe"), with the intention of formalizing the creed. This was one of Judaism's first attempts to introduce dogmas in order to stimulate correct and consistent belief. Although Maimonides was widely accepted, some rabbinic authorities opposed his principles, while still others chose different principles.

Since there is no central rabbinic authority that speaks for

Jews throughout the entire world, it would be difficult to demand a single set of dogmas for all to follow. Interestingly though, the liturgical poem known as Yigdal, often used as a closing hymn in the Friday evening Shabbat service and in some synagogue settings as an opening hymn, consists of thirteen lines which summarize the thirteen principles of faith as formulated by Maimonides.

For many Jews, Judaism is not merely a religion of beliefs. It is very much a religion of action. Some will even say that what one does is more important than what one believes. As the popular saying goes, "Actions speak louder than words."

2. There is no such thing as a Jewish saint

The word "saint" comes from the Latin word *sanctus*, which means "holy." In the Catholic and Orthodox churches, a saint is someone who has been formally canonized as a holy person known for the ability to perform miracles. Saints are able to act as intermediaries between God and people praying to God.

In the Hebrew Bible the root *zdk*, generally translated as "righteousness," occurs more than five hundred times. In the writings of the prophets, righteousness is synonymous with ethical conduct, but not with sainthood in the Christian sense. Although there is no official doctrine in Judaism that would elevate a person to sainthood, there has always been interest in those who have exceptional virtue and faith. Such people are often called *tzaddikim*—people of extreme righteousness. The ancient rabbis often called them *hasidim* —people of exceptional piety, goodness, kindness, and godliness—and some modern scholars translate this term as "saints," although others prefer "pietists." The ancient rabbis discussed the special virtues of the *hasid*, and especially noted that such individuals go well beyond the mere observance of the law. Thus for example, they would prepare for congregational prayer by meditating and concentrating, and would continue to pray long after other worshipers left the congregation to go home.

In medieval Germany, a special type of pietism existed whose saintly followers were known as the Hasidei Ashkenaz, the Pious Ones of Germany. Their ideas and practices are described in the famous book *Sefer Hasidim*, written for the most part by Rabbi Yehudah he-Hasid (Judah the Pious),

who died in 1217. Although written centuries ago, his obser-
vations on the world are strikingly relevant to the contemporary scene. The work addresses subjects ranging from love of
God to how to deal with anger, and scattered throughout the
volume are examples of actual life experiences to illustrate
profound moral lessons.

In the twentieth century the great Bible professor Louis
Ginzberg wrote a book entitled *Students, Scholars and Saints.*
In the book he defines saintliness as "only another word for
heroism in the domain of ethics and religion." He dedicates
a chapter to Rabbi Israel Salanter, the nineteenth-century
rabbi and moralist who best personifies the ideal of the Jewish saint and founded the musar movement for the study of
ethics. Salanter was the kind of man who would always seek
to act kindly to his fellow human beings, even those who
might have wronged him.

In the modern Hasidic movement, which came into being
during the eighteenth century, the tzaddik is looked upon by
his students as the living incarnation of the Torah. The various Hasidic groups have developed different characteristics
in accordance with the particular type of righteous person
to whom they look for guidance. The Hebrew word *tzaddik*
literally means a "righteous person," but when people use the
term today as in "He's a real tzaddik"—they usually mean
"saint."

Today it is perhaps easiest to understand what a tzaddik
signifies in Jewish life by examining the life of Rabbi Aryeh
Levine, one of the great Jewish saints of the past century. In
the book *A Tzaddik in Our Time,* author Simcha Raz records
recollections about Rabbi Levine, known primarily for his
goodness. His main concern was to assist people, never to
judge them. Rabbi Levine's desire to do good was so domi-

nant a passion that he considered it a favor when people allowed him to help them.

An old Jewish tradition, dating back to talmudic times, records that the world is sustained by the presence of at least thirty-six tzaddikim (Sanhedrin 97b, Sukkah 45b). These people do their good deeds quietly, and their neighbors do not know who they are. If, however, that minimum of saintly people does not exist, then the world itself will perish. In Hebrew, the number thirty-six is formed by combining two letters, *lamed* (thirty). and *vav* (six). Even today, one might hear a truly devout, pious, and kind person described as "a real *lamed-vavnik*."

3. The Jews are God's favorite people

The belief that Jews are the chosen people has undoubtedly provoked antagonism from non-Jews. In the 1930s as the Nazis were beginning their mass destruction of Jews, the writer George Bernard Shaw remarked that if the Nazis would only realize how Jewish their notion of Aryan superiority was, they would drop it at a heart beat. After the Yom Kippur War in 1973, Yakov Malik, the Soviet ambassador to the United Nations, remarked that the Zionist theory of the chosen people was tantamount to religious racism. The most antisemitic document in all of world history, *The Protocols of the Elders of Zion,* is based on the idea of an international conspiracy to rule the world by the "chosen people."

In light of these attacks, some Jewish theologians and thinkers wanted to abolish the notion of the Jews as the chosen ones. Rabbi Mordecai Kaplan, founder of the Reconstructionist movement, advocated dropping the chosen theme, not only because it was the model for racist ideology but also because it went against modern thinking to envision the Jews as divinely chosen by God.

It is a myth to think that the Jewish people have been singled out for special favors. Far from it. Chosenness means being selected to carry out the special duties of being God's servant. According to a story in the Book of Exodus, God chose Israel to be a special people when God led them out of Egypt and gave them the Torah on Mount Sinai. God said, "You will be my own treasure from all peoples" (Exodus 19:5). The prophet Isaiah expanded upon the idea of the Jews as chosen by saying: "I have given you as a covenant to the people. For a light unto the nations, to open the eyes of the blind" (Isaiah 42:6–7). This verse is extremely significant. It means that according to Isaiah, the Jewish people were assigned the special mission of improving the world and teaching other peoples to see the light. So Jews must understand that being chosen is not a privilege about which to boast, but rather a responsibility and a task to be undertaken. The Torah never tells us why Jews were chosen, or why Abraham and his descendants were selected for the task of making God known to the world. What God does say is that "it is not because you are numerous that God chose you, indeed you are the smallest people" (Deuteronomy 7:7).

The chosen people idea is such a powerful one that other religious groups have adopted it. Both Protestantism and Catholicism believe that God chose the Jews, but that two thousand years ago a new covenant was made with Christianity. Evangelical Christians often understand chosenness to mean that only Christians go to heaven, while the non-chosen are either damned or placed in limbo.

The Jewish prayerbook reaffirms the idea of chosenness and belief in a special relationship that Israel has with God with these words: "You have chosen us among all the nations; you have loved us and favored us." The same principle of Israel's chosenness is expressed in the words of the blessing one recites when called to the Torah. Jews ought to always be mindful when reciting these words that to be chosen from all the peoples implies added responsibility and obligation, but never thinking of themselves as having the intention to confer feelings of superiority over others. All individuals and groups may enjoy a loving relationship with God, if they choose to.

4. You can't be Jewish if you doubt
God's existence

Questioners often ask whether one can be Jewish and doubt the existence of God. God has an opinion regarding this question. According to the Jerusalem Talmud (Hagigah 1:7), God says, "Better that the children of Israel abandon Me but follow My laws." Thus, according to the rabbis, one can be a good Jew while doubting the existence of God. One should incorporate Judaism's ideals into daily living by studying and practicing Judaism even when one has doubts about God's existence, because Jewish practice and study have spiritual and moral benefits in and of themselves.

The basic Jewish view on this question and one that my own experience has confirmed is that once a person begins to study and live Judaism, he or she will more readily come to the conclusion that God is the ultimate source of morality and life. The Talmud put it this way: "Whereas one may begin to practice Judaism for non-divine reasons, one eventually will become convinced that it represents God's will" (Pesachim 50).

I am reminded of a student I once taught in our confirmation class who very much doubted God's existence. He had trouble praying and did not even want to sign his confirmation certificate, which talked about his affirming his faith in God and the Jewish people. Years later and now a grown man, I met up with this student again when he came back from Texas to visit his family. Curious to know about his life and whether Judaism played any role in it, I proceeded to ask him whether he belonged to a synagogue. He answered, "I love my synagogue. I enjoy working with my kids on their Hebrew school homework, and by the way, I am the president of my shul. And yes, my God beliefs have changed as well!"

5. Jews literally believe in "an eye for an eye"

F ew references in the Jewish Bible are as misused and mis-
understood as the ancient Hebrew law of "an eye for an
eye" (Exodus 21:24). This is often pointed to as an example
of the harsh code of the Israelites. In actuality, however, it
represents a great modification of the even harsher traditions
practiced by the primitive peoples of the Near East before the
Code of Moses. In ancient times, it was customary to treat
the destruction of a vital member of the body as a capital
offense. A person who caused the loss of another's eye was
put to death. The Bible, in contrast, declared that a person
must not suffer greater affliction than he caused, hence the
law "an eye for an eye" and "a tooth for a tooth." The opera-
tive biblical principle was that all punishments by necessity
must be commensurate to the deed.

Throughout history the "eye for an eye" ethic has often
been used and cited to prove the existence of an "Old Testament" ethic of vengefulness, to be contrasted with the New
Testament's supposedly higher ethic of forgiveness and
mercy. An "eye for an eye" is often associated with modern
Jews as well, and invariably in a pejorative manner. The Israeli army, for example, is often chastised in the press for its
"eye for an eye" type of morality when it retaliates against a
terrorist attack.

As biblical tribal life gave way to organized community
living, the Jews of ancient Palestine decided that this principle
was far too severe. The Talmud then reinterpreted the law of
"an eye for an eye" to mean "the cost of an eye for the cost of
an eye." The law was thus understood as requiring monetary
compensation equivalent to the value of an eye. The same

understanding was applied to almost all of the other punishments stated in the same biblical verse, "a tooth for a tooth, a wound for a wound." The guilty person had to pay indemnity for the loss of a limb, much as one does today in accident cases. Any harsher punishments were strictly forbidden. There are many who believe that this is the interpretation originally intended for the biblical phrase "an eye for an eye."

6. Jews literally believe in Satan

There are a number of references to Satan in the Hebrew Bible. In biblical Hebrew, the term *satan* signifies "adversary." It is derived from a verb meaning to oppose and resist. But except for the brief period just before the Christian era, it is doubtful that Jews ever took these references literally. In the course of time, *satan* came to mean pre-eminently the Adversary, the incarnation of all evil, whose thoughts and activities are devoted to the destruction of people. At times *satan* was also identified with temptation, the evil impulse which prompts people to heed the worst side of their nature. But even this notion was never too deep-rooted. For Judaism teaches that God is the Creator of both good and evil, and that God's dominion alone is real.

In the Book of Job, the character of Satan is very real. Satan is portrayed as an adversary who begrudges man's contentment and well-being, and he is the indirect cause of Job's misery.

But the rabbinic sages debated whether the Book of Job was fact or fiction. A number of the most distinguished rabbis contended that the entire Book of Job was actually a product of some ancestor's imagination—a parable or allegory similar to others found in the Bible.

References to *satan* still remain in the Jewish prayerbook, as in the prayer for peace called Hashkevenu. In this prayer there is a sentence which petitions God to "remove from us enemy, pestilence, and *satan*." Here *satan* is generally understood to be synonymous with the evil impulse. It is against the dominance of this impulse that the Jew continues to pray.

It has always been the genius of Judaism to draw on elements of folklore for moral instruction. Among the Jews there persisted vestiges of a primitive belief that the sounding of the shofar (ram's horn) was intended to expel evil spirits. This may well account for Rabbi Yitzchak's explanation (Rosh Hashanah 16b). that the purpose of blowing the *shofar* twice on Rosh Hashanah, the Jewish New Year, is to confound and confuse Satan. Rabbi Yitzchak's comment is reflected in the later practice of reciting before the first series of shofar blasts six biblical verses which form an acrostic of the Hebrew words *kera saatan* ("destroy Satan"). These verses appear in many High Holy Day prayerbooks and continue to be recited in modern times.

In connection with the idea of Satan, an interesting reason for sounding the shofar on the New Year is provided in the talmudic tractate of Rosh Hashanah 16b. There we are told that the purpose of the sounding of the shofar is to confuse Satan, but on the Day of Atonement, Yom Kippur, Satan is completely powerless. This is hinted at in the talmudic book of Yoma 20a where we are told that the numerical value of the Hebrew word *satan* is 364. From this the ancient rabbis deduced that there is one day in the Jewish year when Satan is powerless, and that day is Yom Kippur!

Today many worshipers identify the word *satan* in the prayerbook with the evil impulse. It can serve as a useful reminder of the all-too-frequent human tendency of rationalizing sinful conduct into saintly behavior.

7. The main role of Jewish prophets was to predict the future

In every era it has been believed that some special people could foretell the future. The cult of Nostradamus has its counterparts throughout history. In ancient times, before the great literary prophets of Israel, there were soothsayers and fortune tellers who attempted to predict future events. Beginning around the eighth century C.E, the classical prophets, also known as literary prophets, distanced themselves from these soothsayers. They were called for their mission during a political or social crisis in the community, and their main task was to warn the Israelites, to counsel them, to tell them that if they did not change what they were doing and the way they were doing it, then they would be punished by God. These prophets were prophets because they were able to envision, with help from God, how specific actions would impact the Israelites. Fearlessly, they spoke out and criticized the lack of morality and ethics amongst the Israelites, urging them to raise themselves up to a nobler way of living. They spent their lives condemning judicial corruption, violence, cruelty, arrogance, luxury, greed, and lust for power. They also spent much time attacking those who made cultic worship a priority, because in their eyes the essence of God's demand was to be found in the moral and ethical spheres of life. They thereby introduced the novel concept of morality, whereby worship and its accompanying ritual were means to draw closer to God. For the first time, ritual and its performance became contingent on a person's personal behavior.

The Jewish classical prophets have had a great influence on the Jewish people of today. Many of the ideas of social justice in which Jews have been involved are taken directly from the various books of the prophets. Indeed the Hebrew word for "prophet," *navi*, suggests one who "speaks out," and the prophet was one who predicted not the inevitable, but the most likely consequences of wickedness and violating of God's laws. When the prophet Elijah foretold the tragic climax of Queen Jezebel's life, he was merely reaffirming the principle that one who sows the wind shall reap the whirlwind. And the prophet Jeremiah's prophecies about Jerusalem's doom always had a big "if" attached to them. *If* Judah followed a certain course, then disaster would follow. Thus Judaism wisely rejects the idea that the main role of prophets was their supernatural foresight. Rather, their immortality is based on their inspired insight and their passion for social justice.

8. There is no such thing as the evil eye

The Hebrew *ayin hara* (literally "evil eye"). or *ayn hara* ("evil eye") essentially denote envy, jealousy, and greed. In the Hebrew Bible we are told never to dine with a person who is stingy *(ayn hara)*. and not to desire that person's delicacies. Opposed to the grudging person is the generous person *(tov ayin)*, mentioned in Proverbs 22:9. In the Ethics of the Fathers, a pithy book of rabbinic sayings, we are told (2:13–14) that a good eye (i.e., generosity) is the best quality to which we should cling, and that an evil eye is the worst quality, which we ought to shun.

Over the course of time it became a widespread belief among many Jewish people that an envious or begrudging glance of the eye could work evil upon the person to whom it was directed. Amazingly, the Talmud (Baba Metzia 107b) notes that "ninety-nine out of a hundred die of an evil eye."

The Code of Jewish Law (chapter 23 of Ganzfried's abridged version), considered to be Judaism's most authoritative law code, states that "two brothers, whether of one father or of one mother, may not be called up to the Torah in succession. Nor could a father and son, or grandson be called up in succession, and the reason given is because of the evil eye."

Because of the many warnings of this kind, Judaism developed some ways to ameliorate the deleterious effects of the evil eye. Measures taken to avert the evil eye come in two forms. The first are preventative, where the belief exists that the evil eye is activated by arousing the jealousy of the so-called endowed people. This measure calls for preventative measures of self-restraint, such as the avoidance of expressions of praise for a beautiful newborn baby (who is especially susceptible to the evil eye), wearing a *chamsa* (a specially designed amulet that looks like a hand often containing the evil eye in its center) around your neck, and never mentioning the birth date or exact age of a person.

The other form is counteractive, meaning that once the evil eye has been activated and the threat of danger is imminent, what is needed is not a preventative measure, but rather an immediate confrontation using counter-magic, which works to deceive or ultimately defeat the evil eye. Such measures might include diverting one's glance from the intended target, hanging precious stones between the eyes of the endangered person (Talmud Shabbat 4:5), or qualifying any praise that one gives to a beautiful object or person with the phrase *keyn ayen hore* ("may there be no evil eye"), often shortened to *kaynahora*. No day ever passed when visiting my bubbe Saide when the phrase *kaynahora* was not mentioned. Yes, the evil eye is alive and well in many Jewish households to this very day!

9. Jews believe in heaven and hell

There was a time when the notion of heaven and hell had some currency in Jewish theology. The Hebrew Bible, though making no direct reference to a physical world-to-come, does have some vague poetic allusions to an afterlife. During the period of Persia's dominance over Israel, some of the teachings of Zoroastrianism, including the concept of a heaven or hell in the future world, became popularized among the Jewish people. But even here, heaven and hell were rarely phrased in direct terms. A soul that delighted in a life well lived was spiritually in heaven, while a soul tormented by remorse for its misdeeds was in hell.

Although the word "hell" is not part of the Jewish vocabulary, the Hebrew word *gehinnom* in the Bible is in some circles understood as referring to hell. In fact, it is a term borrowed from an actual place-name, Gei-Ben Hinnom, located south of Jerusalem. It was a valley where the wicked sacrificed their children to false gods. When Jews learned about the concept of hell from their neighbors, they often used this appropriate name to signify the home of the wicked beyond the grave. Over time, Gehinnom passed into use as a metaphoric designation for the place of punishment in the hereafter. Despite the many differences of opinion as to the true meaning of Gehinnom, it is nowhere considered to be dogma or a doctrine of faith that Jews are required to profess.

Heaven is also generally understood metaphorically as God's abode in the skies above. The term does not refer to some good place to which the souls of all deceased persons will return upon their deaths. The Hebrew term *Gan Eden*, Garden of Eden is also used metaphorically as the place where Jews hoped that their deceased loved ones will eventually reside. It is mentioned in the Yizkor memorial prayer for the departed.

Today, it is a fundamental Jewish belief that the soul is immortal, but the precise nature of this immortality is known only to God. It is not part of Jewish faith to accept any literal concept of heaven or hell. In fact, Jews have always been more concerned with this world than the next, and have always believed in concentrating their religious efforts toward building an ideal world for the living.

10. Jews believe that Moses (acting as God's secretary). wrote the first five books of the Bible

The first five books of the Bible are known by the Hebrew term *Torah* (literally "Book of Instruction"). These books are called Genesis, Exodus, Leviticus, Numbers, and Deuteronomy. Since the Torah is also known in Jewish tradition as the Five Books of Moses, many if not most traditional Jews believe that Moses was its sole author, the words themselves having come directly from God's mouth to his ears. By the time the Talmud (the rabbinic interpretation of the Torah) was completed in the year 500 of the common era, some rabbis were already beginning to question whether Moses really wrote certain biblical passages. For instance, it is hard to believe that he wrote the passage in the Book of Deuteronomy that describes his own death.

In the eighteenth century, a Frenchman by the name of Jean Astruc noted that various biblical passages employed different names for God. He also discovered that when the passages containing each name were separated, two parallel accounts of the same story emerged. His discovery (known as the Documentary Hypothesis) earned him a place in history as the father of the scientific study of the Bible.

Today most Bible scholars posit that the so-called Five Books of Moses were the products of schools of people who contributed to its writing. Moses, of course, was one of the contributors. The material was gathered and edited over a span of many centuries, and that is why varying or contradictory statements are found in the Five Books. The more liberal branches of Judaism, including the Reform, Conservative and Reconstructionist movements, have embraced the Documentary Hypothesis as the way the five books of the Torah were created. Traditional Jews do not subscribe to the Documentary Hypothesis.

11. Jews are a race

In pre-Nazi times Jews were often referred to as a race, not only by friends and foes, but by Jews themselves. Antisemites would often speak about the Jews as constituting a distinctive race because they truly believed that the Jewish people had particular genetic qualities that set them apart from others and constituted a threat to society. Hitler clearly saw the Jews as a race, and wrote and commented that as a race Jews possessed inferior Jewish blood.

There is no scientific proof that Jewishness is a race. The history of the Jews reveals countless additions to their numbers through marriage and conversion. There are dark Jews and tall blond ones, Some Jews are short, blue-eyed or brown eyed, and there are Jews whose eyes are dark black. There are many Jews of the white, or Caucasian, race, but there are also black Falasha Jews in Ethiopia, Chinese Jews in Kaifeng, and Indian Jews in Mexico whose origins to this day are mysterious.

A familiar phrase in America says "Funny, you don't look Jewish." Today, both in America and around the world, it would be difficult to tell who is and who is not a Jew. Jews come in a variety of shapes, colors, and physical features. And the genetic differences between Jews in one country and Jews in another can be as substantial as those between non-Jews of the same two countries.

12. Judaism is a religion only

Judaism has often been called the mother religion to Christianity and Islam. In America, Judaism has for the longest time been considered one of the three major religious groups, along with Protestantism and Catholicism. However, it would be a myth to say that Judaism is synonymous with the religion of the Jews. There is no Hebrew word for "religion" in the Bible. The Hebrew word *emunah* means "faith," not "religion." When a Jewish groom places the ring on his Jewish bride-to-be's finger, he utters the Hebrew words *kedat Moshe ve-Yisrael*, meaning "in accordance with the law of Moses and Israel."

Religion is a part of Judaism, but not its totality. In 1934 Rabbi Mordecai Kaplan, founder of the Reconstructionist movement, published his first book, *Judaism as a Civilization*. The book created an explosion in Jewish life and thought, and became the "Bible" of Reconstructionism. In the book Kaplan presents his theory as a kind of Copernican revolution in Jewish thought. Just as Copernicus revolutionized astronomy by arguing that the sun rather than the earth is the center of the universe, so Kaplan suggested that the Jewish people—and not God—should be seen as the center of Jewish life, and everything must be done to preserve the Jewish people even if it means discarding old ideas and values while creating new ones. Kaplan also argued that Judaism includes the whole civilization of the Jewish people—its history, culture, ethical system, language, dance, music, and identification with the land and people of Israel. These are all vital areas embraced by the term Judaism.

One of Kaplan's most important teachings is that Judaism

is a changing, evolving, and developing religious civilization. Religion is the special ingredient that gives our lives meaning, but it is only one part of our whole civilization. Thus, Kaplan argues, the combination of Torah, religion, customs, and culture, the guts of Jewish civilization, will ensure the creative survival of the Jewish people. This definition of the Jewish people as a religious civilization has been accepted today even by Jews who are not part of the Reconstructionist movement.

13. There is no such thing as a black Jew

When I was a rabbinical school student, I used to visit the black synagogue in Harlem. Rabbi Wentworth Arthur Matthew, born in the West Indies, founded the Commandment Keepers Congregation in Harlem in 1919. He trained and ordained many of the black rabbis who later founded synagogues in various places in the United States and the Caribbean.

The emergence of Judaism among people of African descent in the first half of the twentieth century is said to have been made possible by a combination of factors. One was a strong religious tradition in the background of those who became Jewish that embodied Jewish practices from an early but unclear source. When interviewed, many of the older members of this community recalled memories of their parents observing certain dietary laws, such as abstaining from pork. Others recalled traditions related to observing the Sabbath or festivals. In most cases, the practices were fragmentary and observed by people who simultaneously practiced Christianity.

The possible origins of these Hebraic traditions could be traced to West Africa, where a number of tribes have customs so similar to those of Judaism that an ancient connection or maybe even descent from one of the Ten Lost tribes is conjectured. Another possibility for these well-documented practices is association with Jewish slave owners and merchants in the Caribbean and North America.

Many African Americans who practice Judaism today maintain that they have always had a close affinity with the Hebrews of the Old Testament. Scholars such as Albert Raboteau, in his book *Slave Religion*, have described how the biblical struggles of the Hebrew people, particularly their slavery in Egypt, bore a strong similarity to the condition of African slaves and was therefore of special importance to them. This close identification with the biblical Hebrews is clearly seen in the lyrics of gospel songs like the popular "Go Down, Moses."

What all this proves is that there was a foundation, be it psychological, spiritual, or historical, that made some black people receptive to the direct appeal to Judaism that Rabbi Matthew and others made to them.

Rabbi Matthew always maintained that the "original Jews" were black people, or at least non-European. Since his death in 1973, there has been virtually no dialogue between white and black Jews in America.

According to the *Encyclopaedia Judaica*, no reliable statistics exist for the number of black Jewish congregations or for total membership, but estimates suggest there are a few dozen distinct groups in such cities as New York, Chicago, Philadelphia, and Cincinnati, with membership between two and six thousand. Most of these groups consist of individuals who attach themselves to a charismatic figure generally proclaiming a rediscovery of the lost roots of the black nation in Judaism. The groups bear such names as Bnei Israel, Temple of the Gospel of the Kingdom, and Kahal Beth B'nai Yisrael. Their knowledge of Hebrew ritual and the Bible is quite rudimentary.

14. Jews believe the world was created in six days

There are certainly Jewish traditionalists and others who literally believe that the world was created by God in six days, as described in the Book of Genesis. However, many Jews in the Reform, Conservative, and Reconstructionist movements do not understand the creation story literally. And Jewish scholars and many medieval commentators do not consider the details of the biblical account of creation theologically binding.

Evolution and scientific dating do not contradict any of the moral and spiritual views of the biblical creation story, and the numbers in the Bible were rarely if ever taken literally. A single day in the creation story might well symbolize several million years.

For many modern thinkers, the creation story is meant to teach a number of things that one cannot learn from science—for example, that God is a powerful Creator, that the universe is eternal, that the universe was conceived by God's will for a reason and is still evolving according to God's words.

One thing is for certain, and that is that time has not diminished the power or majesty of the biblical creation story. It still moves us, conveying so much in so few words. The opening chapters of Genesis are not a scientific account of the origins of the universe, because the Torah is a book of morality, not cosmology. Its overriding concern is man's relationship to God, offering truth about life rather than truth about science. The creation story describes the world that God fashioned as "good," a statement that no scientific account can make. God's world is an orderly world, in which land and water each have their own domain, in which each species of plant and animal reproduces itself "after its own kind." And at the conclusion of the creation story, man and woman are created and eventually given the freedom to choose how they will act. It is an unfinished world, waiting for us humans to complete God's work of creating.

15. God is a "He" in Jewish prayer

All efforts to describe God are considered to be failures. In Judaism, it is a basic principle of faith that God is without body or form. It is true that the *siddur*, the Jewish prayerbook, has many names for God that imply masculinity. For example, God is called *Av* (Father), *Melech* (King), and Adonai (often translated as "Lord"). If Jews think of God as a male every time they pray using these names for King, they are making the error of literally understanding these terms. But prayer is poetry, and these words are meant to be understood metaphorically. It is not that God is a King, but rather that God has sovereign attributes that resemble those of a King. And God is not a father, but rather has the attributes of a parent. In Judaism, God is not to be understood literally as either a male or a female.

As society continues to grow more egalitarian and inclusive, a new sensitivity has emerged to the God language Jews have always used in prayer, with its previous dependence on masculine imagery. As a result, many of the new prayerbook translations have attempted to eliminate masculine names for God, replacing them with gender-neutral language. For instance, instead of translating the Hebrew words *Avinu malkenu* as "Our Father, our King," prayerbooks often substitute "Our Parent, our Sovereign One."

Interestingly, some feminist prayerbooks use the pronoun "She" for God. A popular feminist metaphor for God in Jewish mystical literature is *Shechinah*, a feminine word always associated with God's nearness either to the people of Israel or to the individual Jew. This "mystical motherly" aspect of God is especially present with Israel in times of tragedy, and it even follows the people into exile. But even here, the feminine side to God is to be understood poetically and metaphorically, never literally. Make no mistake about it—God is neither a He nor a She. In fact, Jewish theologians teach that God is beyond anything conceivable. And that is the mystery of the Godhead.

16. It's not okay for Jews to engage in meditation

S urprisingly, meditation and meditative techniques are actually traditional activities in the Jewish religion. One of the first times we read about meditation in the Bible is in the Book of Genesis. In chapter 24 , Isaac is said to go out into a field to meditate (Genesis 24:63). The rabbinic commentators understood the word "meditate" in this passage to mean "pray," and on the basis of this verse they attributed the afternoon *Mincha* service that Jews recite each day to the patriarch Isaac.

Most people are unaware of the fact that Judaism itself produced an important system of meditation. Since Judaism is an Eastern religion that migrated to the West, its meditative practices may well be those most relevant to westerners. There is considerable evidence that the Jewish mystical masters had dialogue with the Sufi masters and were also aware of the schools of India.

By nature Jews are a spiritual people, and many Jews today are actively seeking spiritual meaning in life, often on a mystical level. Today, many American Jews have become involved in Eastern religions. A large percentage practice disciplines such as transcendental meditation. Until Jews become aware of the spiritual richness of their own tradition, they will continue to search for greener pastures elsewhere.

Meditation has been a part of Jewish prayer and life for the longest time. In the Talmud we read that the early Hasidim would spend an hour before prayer in meditation to direct their minds to God. People are often surprised to now hear the term "Jewish meditation." They have been taught that Judaism is an "in-the-world" religion rather than one that can lead to spiritual transformation. Thus, from an early age many Jews have been given the impression that any technique possibly leading to a spiritual experience is not Jewish and therefore ought to be avoided.

Not too long ago, books on meditation paid little attention to Judaism. Most such books emphasized Eastern practices, and in some instances Christian meditation, but Jewish meditation was for all intents and purposes ignored.

Today, there are many books on Jewish meditation to help Jews (and others who choose to read them) learn the art of meditation.

17. Believing in miracles is essential to being Jewish

Throughout Jewish history, there have been extraordinary events that have had a significant and lasting effect on the Jewish people. The parting of the Red Sea, the heavenly manna that descended in the wilderness providing the Israelites with food, and the cloud of glory showing the Israelites the way through the desert were extraordinary phenomena, to say the least. However, the Bible itself does not deem them miracles. In fact, there is no biblical Hebrew word for "miracle." Instead the Bible uses the words *mofet* ("wonder") and *ot* ("sign"). The Israelites regarded the amazing events in their time as true and authentic. But they did not differentiate between the natural and supernatural, since it was one omnipotent God that caused everything to be and set the course of nature according to God's will. Thus the dividing of the Red Sea and the manna from heaven were accepted as standard historical events, with the Bible itself making no reference to the miraculous nature of these happenings. In God's world there is nothing that is impossible.

Judaism differentiates between hidden miracles and revealing miracles. In rabbinic thinking, a hidden miracle is an occurrence so mundane that its wondrous nature is often overlooked. Hidden miracles are taken for granted as normal events and not as supernatural ones.

Events that cannot be explained and seem to defy the normal scheme of things have never been the major preoccupation of Jewish thinkers. Judaism and its thinkers have been much more interested in the "miracles" that are evident each day: the air we breathe, the daily sunrise and sunset, the beauty of nature's creations. Life itself is considered a hidden miracle, so often taken for granted until illness strikes.

In Jewish liturgical thought, God is viewed as constantly renewing the miracle of creation every day. In the daily prayer known as the Amidah, Jews implore God to keep them mindful of the hidden miracle: "We give thanks and praise You morning, noon and night for Your wondrous miracles which are with us everyday and for Your wondrous kindnesses."

The other type of miracle is the revealing miracle, a powerful, extraordinary, sudden event that contradicts the normal scheme of nature. This is the kind of miracle in which it is believed that God supernaturally intervenes to change the normal course of events. Although Judaism does profess that God is certainly capable of performing this kind of wondrous act, it discourages our desire for God to interrupt God's own laws of nature. Instead, the ancient rabbis have encouraged us to be cognizant each day for the countless miracles that are always with us and to offer words of praise for God's never-failing power.

18. Arguing and debating is un-Jewish

While excessive arguing is not in consonance with Judaism, it is certainly permissible to argue and debate within reason. Much of the Talmud, the first rabbinic interpretation of the Bible, consists of arguments and disputes that various rabbis had in order to determine what would become the law of the land. Though the rabbis showed regard for people of a peaceable nature, such as Aaron the first high priest, they never claimed that we should shun controversy. On the contrary, they felt that controversy was often necessary to sharpen the mind and produce constructive results. Jewish arguing requires us to try to stay kind and humble, making a point of always studying, understanding and valuing all of the positions that are put on the table for discussion.

The Ethics of the Fathers (5:17) differentiates between positive and destructive controversies: "Every controversy which is for the sake of heaven [i.e., spiritually motivated] will endure in the end, but one which is not for the sake of heaven will not endure."

It is not considered proper to argue unfairly. In the Bible a man by the name of Korach became the prototype of controversy and argumentation that was unethical and not for the sake of heaven. Trying to wrest the leadership of the Israelites from Moses, he was a complainer, a grumbler, a power-hungry man who used the power of words as an opportunity to exalt himself above others (Numbers 16). The rabbis advocated that when arguing one focus one's words exclusively on the issue. Use of damaging personal information to invalidate one's adversary, using obscenities and words that hurt, and showing lack of proper decorum is not the proper Jewish way to debate and argue. According to *Sefer Hasidim*, a medieval ethical work that concerns everyday issues, if two people are arguing an issue, one should never say to the other, "You don't know what you are talking about." That kind of language is totally improper, even if the other person is way off the mark. The reason for this prohibition is that saying this phrase to another is tantamount to calling that person a fool, which Judaism strictly forbids.

Jewish advice with regard to the proper way of arguing would likely include being truthful, being slow to anger, being humble, avoiding petty squabbles, giving the other person the benefit of the doubt, and never trying to embarrass another person.

Clearly, the urge to debate issues in Jewish tradition has helped to keep minds sharp and achieve even higher levels of creativity. It has been said that the involvement of Jews in the areas of social reform and politics has been greatly influenced by their training in debate over many centuries.

19. God is completely self-sufficient and does not need people

Since God, unlike human beings, was neither created nor has physical needs in order to be sustained, it is often assumed that God does not really need people. We are in need of God, but God is really not in need of us. This is a wrong assumption, for it ignores God's partnership with man that was entered into at the time of creation. An ancient midrash suggests that the world remained unfinished during the six days of creation so that humans, as partners of God, could complete it. There was an unfinished agenda that has become the agenda of the Jewish people, namely the mending and improving of the world under God's Kingship. God gave the Jewish people six hundred and thirteen biblical command-ments, known as mitzvot, clearly indicating God's need for people to serve as God's partner. Advancing the cause of jus-tice, freedom, and peace are clearly mandates by God to the Jewish people. And even as Jews speak out for all people who are oppressed or persecuted in lands around the world, so too they are bade to speak out on the dangers of nuclear annihila-tion, racism, hunger, and poverty throughout the world, as well as the threats to the environment. By active commitment to the ideals of justice found in biblical and rabbinic law and lore, Jews hope to fulfill their obligation to be partners with God in the creation of a more perfect world.

The theologian Rabbi Abraham Joshua Heschel, the man who marched with Martin Luther King Jr. in 1965 in a march for civil rights, wrote an important book called *God in Search of Man*. In it Heschel discusses God's concern for people and says that man's quest for God presupposes God's quest for man. The awareness of God's interest in man is expressed in Judaism through the idea of the covenant, which God first makes with Abraham, the father of the Jewish people. God needs man for the attainment of God's ends in the world, and Judaism and religion become the vehicle through which man identifies himself with these ends and serves them. This mutual relation imposes a responsibility on God as well as on God's human partners.

A Jewish life is a partnership of God and man, and God is a partner and a partisan in man's struggle for justice, peace, and holiness. God is in need of people for the attainment of God's ends, and religion, as Jewish tradition understands it, is a way of serving these ends. God is indeed in need of man, and man too is in need of God.

20. There is no such thing as a Jewish exorcism

The notion of a foreign spirit or demon entering and possessing the body of a person is known to Christianity for sure, and was popularized by the movie *The Exorcist*. What is surprising is that such a notion is found in Jewish texts of the early talmudic period. The Talmud relates that to help Rabbi Simon bar Yochai have anti-Jewish decrees annulled, a demon entered the body of the emperor's daughter. Upon Rabbi Simon's command, the demon left. Thus was Rabbi Simon ingratiated to the emperor, who then rescinded the edict. Josephus. the great first-century Jewish historian, reports that in his time a Jew named Eleazar drove a demon out of a possessed man in the presence of the Roman emperor Vespasian, by means of putting a certain root to his nostrils and reciting ancient incantations ascribed to Solomon. In the sixteenth century, and even earlier, Jewish exorcism rituals were well known.

CHAPTER 2

Ethics

1. A religious Jew is one who observes commandments

When someone asks "Is so-and-so a religious Jew?" the response invariably is based on the observance of ritual laws: "He keeps kosher and observes the Sabbath; he is religious" or "She does not keep kosher or observe the Sabbath; she is not religious. From such responses one could easily conclude that Judaism regards ethical behavior as an extracurricular activity, something to be desired but not essential. What is at the core of Jewish religiosity?

Today, the Hebrew word *dat* is generally the accepted word for "religion," and a person who is *dati* is understood to be a Jew who scrupulously observes the commandments. Centuries ago, in talmudic times, however, the term that came closest to the definition of religion was *yirat shamayim*, whose translation is "fear of heaven." Religious critics often argue that obedience to God out of fear rarely if ever improves character. And yet, we find many references in the Bible and rabbinic writings to the virtue of fearing God.

Yirat shamayim, the fear of heaven, really denotes a sense of awe in God for whom we have supreme regard. It includes a constant mindfulness to the daily miracles that surround us in life, leading to an urge to fulfill commandments, since that is what God wants us to do. The Torah often uses the phrases "love of God" and "fear of God" interchangeably, implying total devotion to God. For example, "What does Adonai your God ask of you, but to fear Adonai, your God, to walk in all God's ways and to love God and serve God with all of your soul" (Deut. 10:12).

In the popular idiom, saying that a person possesses *yirat shamayim* is simply another way of defining a Jew of piety who is confidently sees himself or herself as fulfilling God's will when performing the mitzvot. Such a pious Jew combines feelings of both love and awe for God, and a desire to fulfill the mitzvot.

In the *Mishneh Torah* (Yesodey ha-Torah 2:2), the medieval philosopher Moses Maimonides conveys the thought concerning true piety in the following terms: When a person contemplates God's great and wondrous works and obtains a glimpse of God's incomparable and wondrous works, that person will surely come to love and glorify God.

Judaism's understanding of God is of a God who wants much more than simple observance of rituals. Ethical behavior is essential, as can be illustrated by God's first question asked in heaven. According to the Talmud (Shabbat 31a), in the hour when a human being is brought before the heavenly court for judgment, he or she is first asked this question: "Did you conduct your business affairs honestly?" God's first concern is human decency, and human decency is a requirement if we are to call ourselves religious.

2. Lying is wrong under all circumstances

All religions extol the virtue of truth. Without truthfulness, morality cannot exist. The Torah leaves no doubt about the fundamental virtue of truth. Exodus 23:7 bids us to "keep far away from falsehood." And from various talmudic sources, we see the value the rabbis placed on telling the truth. "Do not speak what you do not mean in your heart." And the talmudic tractate of Shabbat 55a states that "the seal of the Holy Blessed One is truth." Indeed, all the Jewish moralists are eloquent in advocating truthfulness. As an example, Rabbi Isaac Aboab's *Menorat ha-Ma'or* ("Candelabrum of Light"), in the fourteenth century, quotes Jeremiah 10:10, "Adonai God is truth," and Psalms 119:42, "Your Torah is truth," in its discussion of the virtue of truthfulness (Part II, 2:2). Telling lies in order to mislead others, says Aboab, is a serious offense, but even telling comparatively harmless lies is forbidden.

The ancient rabbis did believe, however, that occasionally a "white lie" is permissible, especially where the intention is to promote peace and harmony (Talmud, Yevamot 65b).

They note that on occasion even God modifies the truth for the sake of peace and harmony. They cite the story in Genesis, chapter 18, when three angels visit the ninety-one-year-old Abraham, to inform him that his eighty-nine-year-old wife, Sarah, will give birth to a child in a year. Standing in a nearby tent, Sarah overhears the comment and laughs to herself, saying, "Now that I am withered, am I to have enjoyment with my husband so old?" A verse later, God appears to Abraham and says, "Why did Sarah laugh, saying, 'Shall I in truth bear a child, old as I am?'" (vv.12–13).

God repeated only part of Sarah's original comment, omitting the words in which she spoke of Abraham as "so old." That comment could have hurt Abraham or made him angry at Sarah. On the basis of this biblical story, the Talmud (Yevamot 65b) concludes, "Great is peace, seeing that for its sake, even God modified the truth."

Yes, there are occasions when a white lie is permissible. Rabbi Judah says in the name of Samuel (Talmud, Baba Metzia 23b–24a) that learned men may conceal the truth regarding three matters: tractate, bed, and hospitality.

Rabbinic commentators explain "tractate" to mean that a scholar is permitted to declare that he is unfamiliar with a tractate of the Mishnah in order not to flaunt his learning. The intent here is for the scholar to preserve a sense of modesty and humility.

"Bed" is understood to mean that if a man is asked intimate questions regarding his marital life, he need not answer truthfully. Such a question is embarrassing and does not deserve a response.

Finally, "hospitality" is understood to mean that a man who has been generously treated by his host may decide not to tell the truth about his reception if he feels that the host will be barraged by unwelcome guests.

People have long debated whether telling a white lie is a departure from truth. There is always the danger that telling white lies can lead to more serious dishonesty. But there are times when Jewish tradition recognizes that a small dishonesty is permissible, especially when the interests of peace are involved.

3. There is no such thing as "finders keepers."

Theft is a serious transgression in Jewish law, especially in light of its being included among the prohibitions in the Ten Commandments. Stealing of every kind is far more prevalent in today's society than we would care to admit. Government statistics indicate that billions of dollars worth of merchandise are being stolen each year.

The Torah has several references to the prohibition of stealing and the penalties for doing so. In addition, there are statements related to the ethical responsibility of the finder of a lost object, For example, the Book of Deuteronomy states that "if you see your neighbor's ox or sheep gone astray, do not ignore it. You must take it back to your neighbor" (Deuteronomy 22:1).

Perhaps the truest test of character lies in the border areas of human behavior. The reaction of a person who finds lost property belonging to another is a good case in point. A finder can easily feel tempted to seek an excuse for retaining the lost article without any sense of guilt, even though such a course of action may amount to robbing a fellow human being. It is for this reason that the Torah considers the return of a lost object to its owner to be a positive mitzvah. According to Jewish law, a Jew must protect the object found and wait for its identification by its rightful owner.

But exactly what is considered lost property according to Jewish law. The Mishnah in Baba Metzia 2:9 states: "If one found a donkey or a cow grazing on the way, this is not lost property. If one however, finds a donkey and its burden topsy-turvy, or a cow running through a vineyard, this is obviously lost property." It is evident in this passage that lost property refers to objects, in this case animals, that are found in places where they obviously are not supposed to be.

In yet another passage in the Mishnah, Baba Metzia 2:1, we learn about articles that when found belong to the finder (i.e., "finders keepers): "If one finds scattered fruit, scattered money, small sheaves in a public thoroughfare, round cakes of pressed figs, a baker's loaves, strings of fish, piece of meat, fleeces of wool which have been brought from the country, bundles of flax and stripes of purple, colored wool—all these belong to the finder." The understanding of this Mishnah by the commentators is that these objects have no defining identification marks that can be used by their rightful owner. Therefore, finders keepers!

The rule of thumb in Jewish law regarding the requirement to return lost property is as follows. When lost property is found and has no telling identification marks, or if a person loses an object (such as a diamond ring that has fallen into the ocean) and then despairs of its ever being returned because of the odds of that happening, then whoever who finds the object is allowed to keep it, with no obligation to seek its rightful owner. Thus, there is such a concept in Jewish law as "finders keepers."

4. It is unethical to assist one's enemy

One would naturally think that we have no obligation whatsoever to our enemy when our enemy is in need. And yet we learn from the Book of Exodus that "if you see your enemy's donkey lying down under its burden and would refrain from raising it, you must nevertheless raise it with him (Exodus 23:5). Here is clear proof that the Torah itself demands that we struggle against natural but unkind human tendencies. The fact that you do not like another person (even considering that person to be an enemy) does not entitle you to ignore the animal's sufferings, let alone those of the person's family members.

In the following midrash (Tanchuma, Mishpatim 1), written in the third century of the common era, we clearly learn how observing the law of helping one's enemy can transform one's kinship with an antagonist:

> Rabbi Alexandri said: Two donkey drivers who despised each other were walking on a road when the donkey of one lay down under its burden. His companion saw it, but at first passed on. But then he reflected: Is it not written in the Torah: "If you see your enemy's donkey lying down under its burden . . . ?" So he returned, and helped his enemy in loading and unloading. He began talking to his enemy: "Release a bit here, pull up over there, unload over here." Thus peace came about between them, so that the driver of the overloaded donkey said, "Did I not suppose that he hated me? But look how kind he has been." Soon, the two entered an inn, ate and drank together, and became fast friends. How did this happen? Because one of them kept what is written in the Torah.

Judaism does not command us to love our enemies, nor does it demand that we hate our enemies. All that is expected of a Jew is to act fairly and equitably, and in some cases, even compassionately toward enemies. As the Book of Proverbs states: "If your enemy is hungry, give your enemy bread to eat" (Proverbs 25:21).

Finally, Jewish scholars differ about whether one should pay a visit to an enemy who falls sick. It is a mitzvah to visit those who are ill and in need of healing. One argument against doing this is that one could create the impression of gloating over another's misfortunes, thereby causing depression in the person being visited. In other words, if it is impossible to convey empathy and concern to a sick person whom one dislikes, it might be best to stay away.

5. Biblical Judaism approved of slavery

Although slavery did exist in ancient Israel, the Bible neither condoned nor encouraged the ownership of slaves. The are striking differences between slavery in ancient Israel and the views of Plato and Aristotle, who influenced Greek society for centuries after the biblical age. Plato encouraged disdain for slaves as a lower class of human being. If a master were to slay his own slave and kill him, all that was required for him to do was to undergo a form of purification. Aristotle viewed slavery as normal and natural, believing that it was human nature that some people should rule others and have powers of ownership over them. In contrast to the beliefs and philosophies of these men, both the Hebrew Bible and the Talmud made no attempt to defend the necessity to hold onto slaves.

What makes the Hebrew slave so special in comparison to slaves in early America is the sensitivity of the Torah to their treatment. The Book of Deuteronomy considers that slaves were virtually members of the master's family, to be included in festival celebrations and sent off with gifts at the end of their period of service. In the Book of Exodus we are told that a master was allowed to chastise a foreign slave, but never in a brutal manner. In fact, there was a penalty for beating him to death: "When a man strikes his male or female slave with a rod so hard that the slave dies under his hand, he shall be severely punished (Exodus 21:20). Rest on the Sabbath and the privilege of participating in the religious life of the family circle were not to be denied by an Israelite owner. Fugitive slaves were given asylum, for Deuteronomy 23:16 states that "you shall not return a runaway slave to his master." The slave went free if the master destroyed his eye or tooth. Freed slaves had the status of proselytes in every respect.

The Hebrew slave, on the other hand, was in a much more favorable position. He became a slave either by selling his services in order to obtain maintenance or through inability to pay his debts. The male worked for a six-year period and was then released. And all Hebrew slaves, both those who had chosen to remain with their masters when the seventh year came and those who had served six years, were released at the year of Jubilee (Leviticus 25:40), whether or not they preferred to serve their masters. This clearly shows that the Torah was not really in favor of slavery.

There is no evidence that slave markets ever existed in Israel. Kidnapping a man or selling him as a slave was a capital offense. According to the Talmud (Kiddushin 20a), a slave was to be regarded as his master's equal. By the eleventh century, the great philosopher Maimonides wrote in his *Mishneh Torah*, Laws of Slavery 9:8, that "it is permissible to make a Canaanite slave work with rigor, but the ways of ethics and prudence require that the master should be just and merciful, not to make the burden too heavy on his slave and not press him too hard. One should not shout or be angry with them, but listen to their complaints.

Because the Torah is sensitive to the treatment of slaves, and because the Jews were enslaved as strangers in Egypt for so many years, the Torah states on more than thirty occasions the importance of treating strangers with respect and compassion. Exodus 22:20 says: "You shall not wrong a stranger or oppress him, for you were strangers in the land of Egypt."

Slaves, like strangers, are human beings created in God's image, and that is why a slave's status could never be reduced to mere property. And furthermore, the Torah saw the desired state of man as free, for that is the central message of the first half of the Book of Exodus. Thus, if a slave risked his master's anger by running away, the Torah's sympathies were exclusively on the side of the slave. The contemporary upshot of the biblical verse requiring a runaway slave to remain free is that democracies should be generous in granting political asylum to people fleeing totalitarian regimes.

CHAPTER 3

Hebrew and Jewish Expressions

1. A mitzvah is a good deed

While you might hear Jews refer to doing a mitzvah as meaning doing a good deed or some other kind act (such as "I did a mitzvah today and helped a shut-in by bringing him food"), a mitzvah is much more than that. In Judaism, a mitzvah is an act that is performed in accordance with God's will. The Hebrew word *mitzvah* (plural *mitzvot*). means "religious instruction" or "commandment." It refers to a religious obligation or duty established by the rabbis who lived centuries ago.

In the talmudic period all of the biblical precepts and prohibitions found in the Five Books of Moses were grouped in categories. Generally, we say that there are 613 commandments in the Torah, although scholars disagree on the actual list. There are 248 positive mitzvot ("You should do") and 365 negative ones ("You should not do"). It was Rabbi Simlai, a Palestinian scholar, who first gave the figure of 613 for the commandments revealed to Moses at Mount Sinai. The 613 commandments range from commandments required only of the high priest in the Temple to a simple acts of kindness to be performed by all of us, such as visiting the sick. In his *Sefer ha-Mitzvot* ("Book of Commandments"), written in 1170 C.E, the philosopher Moses Maimonides cites the sources of all the mitzvot in the Torah and teaches his readers about them.

Mitzvot are further categorized in a variety of other ways. For example, there are mitzvot that are bound to specific times (e.g., wearing a tallit during prayer only in the morning) and mitzvot that can be observed any time of day or year (e.g., helping the poor, caring for animals). The Jewish sages also made a distinction between mitzvot that were classified as "light" (i.e., less important) and those that were classified as "heavy" (more serious). For example, Maimonides classified the act of celebrating a festival as a light mitzvah and the mitzvah of learning Hebrew as a heavier one.

Not all mitzvot are designed for the mind. Many are intended for the soul. The rabbis also distinguished between commandments for which the reason for doing them was easy to figure out, what we may call "rational," as compared to mitzvot that seemed less logical, often called "nonrational." Most of what we might call ethical mitzvot, such as "do not steal" or "do not kill," are rational commandments. Keeping the Jewish dietary laws of kashrut is an example of a non-rational mitzvah.

The rabbis also made a distinction between commandments that help people relate to one another and those that help people in their relationship to God. People-to-people mitzvot, as many like to call them, include the prohibitions regarding jealousy and theft of things your neighbor owns. Eating in a sukkah or putting a mezuzah on one's doorpost are some of the mitzvot that connect a person to God.

Finally, the rabbis taught that there are seven commandments that were given to Adam and Noah in the Book of Genesis that all people should observe, whether Jewish or not. These include the prohibitions against blasphemy, idolatry, incest, bloodshed, robbery, murder, and eating flesh cut from a living animal, and a positive commandment requiring the establishment of courts of justice.

Although the Torah on several occasions builds in a reward for doing a mitzvah (e.g., long life for honoring parents), the ancient rabbis advised that we are to perform the commandments not for the sake of the reward, but rather to know the satisfaction that mitzvot bring to one's life. Observing commandments carries a cumulative spiritual reward.

2. *Mazal Tov* means "Good luck"

M any of the ancient rabbis felt that luck often plays an important role in shaping our lives. The Hebrew phrase *mazal tov*, often translated as "good luck" or "congratulations" reflects this rabbinic thought. "Mazal tov" is the traditional greeting at Jewish weddings, circumcisions, anniversaries, and any festive or happy occasion. Thus, for example, when I was about to defend my doctoral thesis at Columbia University, many of my friends said to me, "We wish you *mazal,* and we hope things go well for you." In fact, the Hebrew phrase *mazal tov* actually means "lucky star." The biblical word *mazal*, occurring in II Kings 22:5, has been understood to mean either a planet or a sign of the zodiac. In talmudic literature, *mazal* signifies "star of fortune" or "fate" or "destiny." The meaning of mazal tov today as "congratulations" is a survival of the ancient Jewish belief in astrology. Many ancient people, including the Egyptians and the Babylonians along with the Jews, believed that the position of the stars had special powers over people and could influence their destiny. Hence the word *mazal* assumed the meaning of fortune or fate to which people were subjected. Inherent in the greeting "mazal tov" is the wish that the event being celebrated take place "under a lucky star."

Interestingly, during the early days of Jewish history, there seems to have been a belief that human destiny was linked to the motion of the stars. The prophet Jeremiah was one of the first biblical spokesmen to condemn this notion as pagan, and centuries later the philosopher Moses Maimonides renewed the attack on astrology. He declared that astrology is not only forbidden, but borders on idolatry. But long after the origin of the phrase was lost, "mazal tov" continued to mean, "May your life be crowned with good fortune.

Among Sephardic Jews, the expression *siman tov,* meaning "good sign or omen," is frequently extended to celebrants. And the Yiddish language adopted several expressions derived from *mazal*: *mazeldig* (lucky), *shlimazel* (a person without luck), and *shlimazeldig* (unlucky).

And yet Judaism is not a fatalistic religion, and the Jews rejected the popular belief among the ancients Greeks and followers of certain other Oriental faiths that people have no control over their own destiny. In the Ethics of the Fathers (3:19), the rabbis declare that "Everything is foreseen, yet freedom of choice is given." Freedom to choose is humanity's gift from God. We may have no say as to the cards that are dealt us in life, but we have the freedom to choose how to play our cards. The decision about how to play them lies in our hands.

3. Tzedakah and charity are synonymous

There is no doubt that many Jews understand the Hebrew term *tzedakah* to mean "charity," but this meaning in no way conveys all that tzedakah truly denotes. To better understand the concept of tzedakah, one has to look at its root meaning. Its derivation is from the biblical word *tzedek*, which means "justice" or "righteousness." In post-biblical Hebrew tzedakah specifically applies to the relief of poverty as an act of justice and moral behavior. The use of tzedakah to designate any work directed toward assisting the poor signifies that the poor person's right to food, clothing, and shelter is considered by Judaism as a legal claim that must be honored by the more fortunate. The word "charity," on the other hand, comes from the Latin word *caritas*, referring to the love of one person for another. It is true that Jews give tzedakah because they know that helping the poor is a loving and kind thing to do. But there's more. Jews do tzedakah because that act helps to eliminate injustice in the world. Thus, tzedakah is the righteous way to give.

In Judaism, tzedakah is required of all people, rich and poor. No matter where a person is in life, there is always another person less fortunate. In his *Mishneh Torah*, Maimonides devotes ten chapters to Gifts to the Poor and the rules and regulations related to this subject. He writes: "Anyone who can afford it must give charity to the poor according to their needs. One's first duty lies toward his poor relatives, then toward the needy of his own town, and finally toward those of other towns." Maimonides also created a famous scale of eight degrees of contributors. The lowest degree is the person who gives grudgingly, whereas the highest degree of tzedakah is to assist a person by offering a loan, or by entering into partnership with him, or by providing work for him, so that the recipient becomes self-supporting.

Rabbi Israeli al-Nakawa of fourteenth-century Spain writes in his *Menorat ha-Ma'or* ("Lamp of Illumination") that the world is like a revolving wheel. One who is rich today may be poor tomorrow. Therefore we should give tzedakah before the wheel turns. Prominent Jews in France used to make their coffins out of the tables on which they served food to the poor, to show that a man can take nothing with him except the good he has done.

In modern times the giving of tzedakah though large agencies such as the Jewish Federation's United Jewish Communities has changed the whole method of giving tzedakah. The collection of large funds by combining contributions has proven to be effective in helping many different causes. But Jewish law says that even if one has already given to a Jewish community campaign, it is still forbidden to turn away anyone seeking help. As the Book of Deuteronomy states: "Justice, justice, shall you pursue" (Deuteronomy 16:20). The Talmud goes one step further in telling of the importance of tzedakah when it states that "charity is equal to all the other commandments combined!" (Baba Batra 9b).

4. Kosher means eating food that meets Jewish legal standards

Although kosher is often understood to mean foods that are okay for Jews to eat, the Hebrew word *kasher* from which the word "kosher" is derived means "that which is proper or fit, the correct way to do something according to Jewish law and tradition." That is why one can ask about a business dealing of questionable legality, "Is it kosher?" Similarly, one might say of the parchment in a mezuzah whose Hebrew letters are beginning to fade due to excessive wear, "Is it kosher?" meaning, "Is it fit to be used according to Jewish law?"

When something is not kosher, Jewish tradition generally uses the words *treif* or *pasul*. A Torah scroll, for example, if improperly written or in disrepair, is considered non-kosher. Similarly, a tallit (prayer shawl) that is missing one of the four fringes required on each of its corners is also considered non-kosher and therefore unacceptable to wear according to Jewish law. Food that is not kosher and by definition not permitted to be eaten according to Jewish law is referred to as *treif* food.

Although the Hebrew word *kasher* (or "kosher" as we hear it in English) is generally associated in Judaism with food and dietary restrictions, the word appears only once in the entire Hebrew Bible. In the Book of Esther, which is read on the holiday of Purim, the word *kasher* appears in chapter 8, verse 5. Queen Esther beseeches King Ahasuerus to avert the evil that Haman has plotted against the Jews. "Esther said: 'If it pleases the king, and I have found favor in his sight, and the proposal seems proper (*kasher*), and if I am pleasing to you—let dispatches be written to revoke the letters concocted by Haman which he issued, ordering the destruction of the Jews in all the provinces." In this context there is no doubt that kosher means "fit" or "proper."

For the traditional Jew, kosher is more than just the food. Meticulous Jews who wish to keep all Jewish rituals aspire to live a kosher life, carefully caring for observance, and living each day and seeing it through Jewish eyes.

5. Jews originated the phrase "People of the Book" by which they are known

J udaism obligates its people to study the Torah and the
other books of the Hebrew Bible. Their acceptance of the
Five Books of Moses marked the birth of the Hebrew people.
These five books became their books of instruction, and centuries ago the rabbis mandated that the Torah was to be read
every Monday and Thursday (ancient market days), as well
as on Saturdays (the Jewish Sabbath) and on all festivals.

No one is exempted from Torah study, even the king: "And
it shall be that when he sits on the throne of his kingdom that
he shall write a copy of this law in a book. And it shall be
with him, and he shall read therein all the days of his life"
(Deuteronomy 17:18). Moses's successor, Joshua, was also
instructed to apply himself to the Torah: "This book of the
law shall not depart from your mouth, but you shall meditate
in it day and night, that you may observe to do according to
all that is written in it" (Joshua 1:8).

According to Moses Maimonides, every Jew is required to
study Torah, whether rich or poor, healthy or ailing, young
and strong or old and feeble. "Until what period in life is
one obligated to study Torah? Until the day of one's death"
(*Mishneh Torah*, Laws of Torah Study). The Ethics of the
Fathers advised regarding the reading of the Torah: "Turn it
over and over again, for one can find everything in it" (Ethics
of the Fathers 5:22).

The biggest myth is that the Jews gave themselves the name
"People of the Book." Surprisingly, it was Mohammed (the
founder of Islam), about fifteen hundred years ago, who is
credited with naming the Jews the People of the Book. The

book to which he was referring was, of course, the Bible. This is a theological term primarily related to Islam, and it designates a people who according to the Koran received God-revealed Scriptures. For Muslims the Koran is the completion of the Scriptures.

Today the Hebrew term *Am ha-Sefer* ("People of the Book") has become a self-applied term and refers specifically to the Jewish people and the Torah. Indeed, the life and destiny of Jews has been formed not only by the Bible but by all of the many books inspired by the Bible. The eleventh-century philosopher Moses ibn Ezra wrote in his *Shirat Yisrael* that "a book is a friend who will cause you no harm and deny you no favor. If you fall upon evil times it will be a friend in your time of loneliness, a light in your darkness. It gives all and takes nothing." And the modern Rabbi Harold Kushner in his book *To Life* (p. 40). has written that "Jews read the Bible the way a person reads a love letter. When you read a love letter, you don't just read it for content. You try and squeeze ever last little bit of meaning out of it."

CHAPTER 4

Jewish Holidays

1. Hanukkah is a major Jewish festival

Hanukkah is one of North American Jewry's most popular holidays, if not the most popular. In fact, the most recent demographic surveys indicate that nearly 90 percent of North American Jews report lighting Hanukkah candles, while fewer than 40 percent light Sabbath candles. If the current trend continues, Hanukkah may overtake attending the Passover Seder as the most observed Jewish celebration. With that kind of participation, it would surely seem that Jews themselves envision Hanukkah as one of Judaism's most important holidays. Hanukkah's good fortune in the Western world results from its proximity to Christmas. Because the holiday begins on the 25th of Kislev, and because the Jewish calendar is lunar, this means that Hanukkah can occur any time between the end of November up until the end of December. And because Western Jews live in a predominantly Christian society, and because of its proximity to Christmas, some Jewish parents have converted Hanukkah into a Jewish version of Christmas, including the giving of gifts on all eight nights. But of course the only really required ritual act is to light candles each night and recite blessings. The ceremony is completed in just a few minutes. It's very easy to observe.

But it's a myth to think that Hanukkah is a major Jewish holiday. In fact, Jewish tradition relegates the festival of Hanukkah to the status of a minor holiday. In Jewish law, Hanukkah is considered less significant than the Sabbath, or Rosh Hashanah, Sukkot, Passover, and Shavuot. All the major holidays are mentioned in the Torah, whereas Hanukkah is not. Work is prohibited on all major holidays, whereas on Hanukkah there are no work restrictions. An elaborate liturgy is associated with the major Jewish holidays. Hanukkah has a few additional prayers inserted into its daily liturgy, but nothing compared to the extra ones on major festivals. In the Talmud, Hanukkah is given limited press. The talmudic discussion begins with the question "What is Hanukkah?" It appears as if the answer was not very well known when the Talmud was completed in the fifth century of the common era. It has been conjectured that the compiler and editor of the Mishnah, Rabbi Judah the Prince, who claimed to be a descendant of King David, regarded the priestly Hasmonean family (the Maccabees) as usurpers since they were not descended from the Davidic line and therefore were not entitled to rule over Israel.

Today in the State of Israel Hanukkah is often celebrated as a patriotic holiday, with the military heroism of the Maccabees serving as a source of inspiration to the Israeli army and its soldiers.

Although Hanukkah is rabbinically considered a minor holiday, it does have an important major lesson, namely the importance of continuing to fight for religious freedom for all people and for the right to be different. This is why Hanukkah ought to be one of the most popular of Jewish holidays— but only if its true meaning and importance inform its celebration.

2. Yom Kippur is the only fast-day in the Jewish year, and the saddest one too

The erroneous perception of Yom Kippur, the Day of Atonement, as the saddest day in the Jewish calendar is largely due to it being a day of fasting. The goal of the holiday, though, is not self-affliction, but rather to bring about reconciliation between people and between people and God. Concerning the character of Yom Kippur, the ancient rabbis said: "There were no days as happy for the Jewish people as the fifteen of the month of Av [a day of arranged marriages] and Yom Kippur" (Mishnah Taanit 4:8).

Another popular *bubba meise* about the Day of Atonement is that if one prays all day in synagogue with fervor and intention, then forgiveness by God for all of one's sins will be the result. In fact, the only sins forgiven on Yom Kippur are those committed against God. As for transgressions committed against other people, the rabbis say: "Yom Kippur does not atone until one appeases his neighbors" (Mishnah Yoma 8:9).

Given the life-and-death issues that rule the roost on Yom Kippur, we might ask why the Talmud regarded it as a happy day. Perhaps, because at the end of the day Jewish people experience a great catharsis and feeling of serenity, a feeling that comes with the knowledge that if they have prayed with proper feeling and intention they have made peace with their friends and God.

As for the saddest day in Jewish history, it is the ninth of Av, which falls sometime between July and mid-August. On this day the Babylonians destroyed the First Temple in 586 B.C.E. and the Romans burned the Second Temple in 70 C.E. The events commemorated by this fast-day, known in Hebrew as Tisha B'Av, were so horrific that Jewish law ordains that Jews are to refrain from most pleasurable activities from the beginning of the month during which Tisha B'Av falls. And on the Ninth of Av itself, the rabbis ordained a day of not eating or drinking, not bathing, and no makeup or perfume or sexual relations.

There are yet other minor fast-days throughout the Jewish year, in addition to Yom Kippur and the Ninth of Av. They are called minor because they are only half-fast-days, where food is forbidden only from dawn till evening. Three of the minor fasts are observed in memory of the destruction of the two Temples. The Tenth of Tevet fast (usually in January) commemorates the beginning of the Babylonian siege of Jerusalem. During the summer, traditional Jews observe the fast of the Seventeenth of Tammuz, the day Roman troops breached the walls of Jerusalem in 70 C.E. A third minor fast is the Fast of Gedaliah, occurring the day after Rosh Hashanah and commemorating the assassination of the Jewish governor Gedaliah whom the Babylonians installed to rule over Judea. Yet a fourth minor fast is the Fast of Esther, occurring on the day before Purim, commemorating Esther's three-day fast in the Book of Esther. A final fast is obligatory for only a small percentage of Jews—the fast of the firstborn males. This fast begins on the eve of Passover, and commemorates the tenth plague that God inflicted on the Egyptians, the killing of firstborn sons.

The rabbis cited in the talmudic tractate of Berachot said that "the merit of a fast is the charity it produces." This may be a good reason for Jews who have never attempted to observe many of these minor fasts to try their hand at doing so, for who would not want to fulfill an opportunity to bring charity into one's life?

3. Physical exertion is prohibited on the Sabbath

The Torah explicitly says that "the seventh day is the Sabbath unto God, and in it you shall do no manner of work" (Exodus 20:10). Taking this verse literally, it appears that all manner of work is strictly forbidden on the Sabbath. Less familiar to most people is the rabbinic definition of work. For instance, Jewish law forbids turning on an oven or stove, which few people would regard as doing work. Yet Jewish law disallows it. On the other hand, Jewish law does not prohibit moving a heavy object in your home from one room to another on the Sabbath, although such moving is surely physical exertion.

The Hebrew word for prohibited work is *melachah*, which Rabbi Abraham Chill, in his compelling book *The Mitzvot* (p. 37), has defined as "any labor involving the production, creation or transformation of an object." One can spend the entire Sabbath moving heavy objects from one room to another in one's home and not violate the holy Sabbath, whereas the striking of a match to light one's fireplace is considered a desecration because it involves creation.

The rabbis in talmudic times formulated the definition of work prohibited on the Sabbath by enumerating thirty-nine major and other secondary classifications of work that constitute a violation of Jewish law. Since the description of the Sabbath in the Torah is juxtaposed immediately before the construction of the Tabernacle, the rabbis concluded that there was a logical rational connection between the two, namely that all categories of work performed on the Tabernacle were meant to be disallowed on the Sabbath. Additionally, there are other categories of work that the rabbis caution Jews to avoid because they are not in the so-called spirit of the Sabbath. For instance, discussing business matters or reading business correspondence would fall into this category.

In addition, Jewish law requires us to avoid doing anything on the Sabbath that might lead to a prohibited act. The example here would be that since spending money on the Sabbath is forbidden, we should not even handle money on the Sabbath.

Thus the common belief that any manner of work, especially strenuous physical work, is strictly forbidden on the Sabbath is a myth. It all depends on whether the work in question falls into one of the thirty-nine categories enumerated by the rabbis.

In enacting the laws which prohibited some types of work on the Sabbath, the rabbis were clearly interested in making the Sabbath day a day in which Jews can relieve themselves from the tension and competition of weekly chores and rejuvenate themselves both physically and spiritually. Rabbi Abraham Joshua Heschel said it very well when he wrote in his book *The Sabbath*, "Six days we seek to dominate the world, and on the seventh day to dominate the self" (p. 13).

4. You can drink to yours heart's content on Purim

One of the strangest rabbinic statements is associated with the festival of Purim. It enjoins that Jews are to get so drunk that they can not tell the difference between "Blessed is Mordechai" and "Cursed is Haman." (Talmud, Megillah 7b). This is the only instance of an injunction to get drunk in the whole of Jewish literature. It stems from the fact that Purim is one of Judaism's most joyous holidays, commemorating the defeat of the evil Haman. Most of the commentators argue that it was not, in fact to be taken literally. Nonetheless, a considerable number of Jews do get drunk on Purim, using the rabbinic advice offered centuries ago as their justification.

It is true that drinking wine (or grape juice) is an imperative in Judaism for celebrating holy days. This imperative is based on the verse in Psalms which says that "wine gladdens the heart." But Jewish sources have always recognized heaviness of limbs, difficulty in focusing, and impaired judgment as potential effects of alcohol consumption. Princes, judges, teachers, and ritual slaughterers must remain sober according to Jewish law in order to carry out their duties. And according to the Jerusalem Talmud (Terumot), a person who has been drinking alcohol in any amount faces restrictions in joining in communal prayer.

Because of its effects on the brain and central nervous system, alcohol is considered a drug. For teenagers today, it is the drug of choice. Driving under the influence can be very risky and has led to serious accidents and many deaths. Today's medical opinion states that excessive alcohol consumption can not only lead to physical addiction, but can increase the risk of heart attack, stroke, brain damage, liver disease, and several types of cancers.

Because the Torah says "Take heed and guard your lives carefully" (Deuteronomy 4:9). Jewish law requires us to take care of our bodies. The Code of Jewish Law mandates that we are to remove any object or obstacle that constitutes a danger or potential danger to life. Because there are so many recovering alcoholics and people with other health problems, most Jewish authorities would recommend not taking the talmudic verse about getting drunk on Purim literally. Rather, rabbinic authorities urged us to steer a middle course. Drunkenness is held to be wrong and un-Jewish, but a complete rejection of alcohol is not advocated. We are permitted to drink, but how many drinks we have is left for us to decide as free human beings aware of the perils of alcohol to our health. According to the great medieval philosopher Nachmanides in his commentary to the Torah, this is implied in the verse "Speak to the children of Israel and say to them: You shall be holy, for I Adonai your God am holy" (Leviticus 19:2). Nachmanides points out that certain things are categorically forbidden by the Torah, but the command to be holy implies that we must not overindulge even in those things that are permitted. For Jews, taking the course of moderation is always the preferred choice.

5. Rosh Hashanah occurs in the first month of the Jewish calendar

M any people quite naturally but mistakenly assume that that Rosh Hashanah, the Jewish New Year, falls in the first month of the Hebrew calendar. The strange fact is that the Jewish New Year, Rosh Hashanah, actually takes place in Tishrei, the seventh month of the Hebrew calendar. It is as if the Western world's secular New Year were to be celebrated on July 1 rather than January 1.

The first month of the Hebrew calendar is actually the month called Nisan. In this month, the Jewish people were freed from four hundred years of Egyptian slavery. In Exodus 12:1 it says: "God said to Moses and Aaron in the land of Egypt: This month [i.e., Nisan] shall mark for you the beginning of the months. It shall be the first of the months of the year for you." One of the first steps in the process of liberation was for the Israelites to have their own calendar, their own way of keeping track of time and recalling the most salient events of their history. Thus the Torah wanted the beginning of the months to mark the time that the Israelites gained their freedom from Egyptian bondage.

Rosh Hashanah, the Jewish New Year, actually occurs on the first day of the seventh month, Tishrei. Rabbinically speaking, it traditionally marks the creation of the world. Medieval Jewish writers noted that the Hebrew letters of the word *bereshit* ("in the beginning") with which the Book of Genesis begins the account of creation could be arranged to read *alef be'tishrei* ("the first day of the month of Tishrei"), when the Jewish New Year is celebrated. The Talmud emphasizes the importance of Rosh Hashanah not only as the birthday of the world, but also as the festival commemorating some of the most dramatic events in Israelite history. God remembered Sarah on the first day of Rosh Hashanah, Isaac was born on Rosh Hashanah, Hannah was remembered on Rosh Hashanah and her son Samuel was the answer to her prayers at the sanctuary of Shiloh.

Whereas most Jewish holidays celebrate national events in Jewish history (e.g., Passover commemorates the Jewish exodus from Egypt), Rosh Hashanah celebrates the birthday of the world and allows Jews to do some self-assessment by examining their mistakes and misdeeds.

6. There is only one Jewish New Year celebration in the Hebrew calendar

M ost Jews think of Rosh Hashanah as the one and only Jewish New Year. Although it is one of the most observed and celebrated one, there are, surprisingly, several other new years which Jews also are enjoined to celebrate. For example, just as Jewish tradition regards the first day of Tishrei as the New Year for mankind, so too it regards the fifteenth day of the month of Shevat as the New Year for trees (called Tu Beshevat). This holiday falls between mid-January and mid-February, and is celebrated in Israel by planting trees. Many North American and European Jews commemorate the holiday of Tu BeShevat by contributing to the Jewish National Fund, which uses the dollars to develop forests throughout the State of Israel. There is also a seemingly growing tradition on Tu BeShevat to have a special Seder that is modeled largely on the Passover Seder. This tradition was initiated by Jewish mystics, and includes drinking four cups of wine and reading Bible passages that relate to vegetation.

Two other Jewish New Years (observed in bygone years) are specified in the Mishnah (Rosh Hashanah 1). The first of the two is on the first of Nisan, which corresponds to the season of the redemption from Egypt and the birth of the Israelite nation. The first of Nisan is also the New Year for the reigns of Jewish kings . And the last of the new years, the first of Elul, is the New Year for the tithing of cattle. The tithe for cattle had to be made from cattle born in the same fiscal year, between the first of Elul one year and the next.

These four different Jewish New Years were established to ensure that commandments were completed at their appointed times, and to provide boundaries and markers for a variety of activities. So be reminded that in addition to wishing your friends and family a Happy New Year on Rosh Hashanah, there are three other occasions in the year when you will have opportunities to do so.

7. Rosh Hashanah is sometimes late, sometimes early

Each year, depending on the date of Rosh Hashanah, one often hears the words "Rosh Hashanah is so late this year," or alternatively, when Rosh Hashanah falls in early September, "I can't believe how early Rosh Hashanah is this year." The fact is that the Jewish calendar is based on a lunar year, running 354 or 355 days, rather than the solar year of the Gregorian calendar, which runs 365 or 366 days. Jewish holidays will always fall on the same date of the Jewish calendar, and for Rosh Hashanah that date is the first of the Jewish month of Tishrei. But because the lunar calendar loses days to the solar calendar each year, the date of Rosh Hashanah in the civil calendar will vary, sometimes falling in September, and other years in October. In order for the deviation in time not to be so very great, seven times in nineteen years an entire additional month (Adar II) is added to the Jewish calendar. This leap month occurs approximately every three years, and is meant to keep the holidays in synchronization with their seasons. But according to the Jewish calendar Rosh Hashanah is never late or early. It's always at the beginning of the Jewish year, and will never deviate from falling on the first of the month of Tishrei.

8. Hanukkah gelt has no historical basis

In many Jewish households, gifts are given on Hanukkah. Small gifts of money, known as Hanukkah gelt, are especially popular. In keeping with this tradition, many kosher candy companies craft chocolate candy in the shape of coins, and these too are exchanged as gifts. Coins from the time of the Maccabees were depicted on the first postage stamps of the State of Israel, to commemorate the victory of the brave Maccabees over the Syrian Greeks, which allowed Jews freedom of religion.

In 1958 the Bank of Israel initiated a program of striking commemorative coins for use as Hanukkah gelt. The first Hanukkah coin portrayed exactly the same menorah that had appeared on the last Maccabean coins of Antigonus some two thousand years earlier. In 1976, the year of America's bicentennial and the two-hundredth year of independence, the Hanukkah coin featured a colonial menorah. So the giving of Hanukkah gelt today surely does have some historical precedents.

CHAPTER

Death and Dying

1. The Mourner's Kaddish is a prayer for the dead

The understanding that the Mourner's Kaddish is a prayer for the dead stems from the custom requiring its recitation at worship services after the death of a parent. What surprises most people about the Mourner's Kaddish is the fact that nowhere in the prayer is there any reference to death and dying. The main thrust of the prayer is clearly indicated in its opening words, *Yitgadal ve'yitkadash shmay rabbah*—"Glorified and sanctified be the name of God." These words were adopted from the Book of Ezekiel (38:23), in which God says *Ve-hitgadalti ve-hitkadashti* meaning—"I will manifest My greatness and My holiness." In response to the first words of the Kaddish, the congregation says *Y'hay shmay rabba mevorach*—"May God's name be blessed." These words are taken almost verbatim from Daniel 2:20.

The question, then, is why this prayer was designated by Jewish law to be recited by the bereaved in honor of their loved ones. It is likely that people recited the Kaddish because it honored the deceased by testifying that he or she had left behind noble descendants, people who attended daily services and proclaimed their continuing loyalty to God by magnifying God's name.

The earliest reference to the Kaddish serving as a prayer for mourners is found in *Or Zarua*, a book by the twelfth-century Rabbi Isaac ben Moses of Vienna. The next reference to it appears in the *Machzor Vitry*, dated 1208, where we read: "The boy rises and recites the Kaddish." Undoubtedly, the rabbis of old regarded the Kaddish as the perfect prayer for mourners, whose faith is being tested by the loss suffered.

By the thirteenth century, reciting the Mourner's Kaddish for the departed was encouraged by Jewish mystics, who contended that the prayer had the power to redeem the souls of the deceased.

Jewish law only requires sons of the deceased to recite the Mourner's Kaddish. Where there are no sons, daughters are not required to say Kaddish. Orthodox custom often suggests that the daughter honor her deceased parents by responding "amen" as others recite the Kaddish. There are modern Orthodox authorities who do not discourage a woman from reciting the Kaddish for a loved one. Reform rabbis often encourage all congregants to rise during the reciting of the Mourner's Kaddish as a symbolic show of solidarity for the bereaved. Judaism also regards anyone, even someone who was not a relative of the deceased, to recite the Kaddish for a deceased person as an act of kindness.

For the Jewish mourner of today, the recitation of the Kaddish, although it makes no reference to death or the departed loved one, is helpful in that it focuses the mourner on life and the living in the midst of sorrow. In addition, because reciting the Mourner's Kaddish requires a minyan (a quorum of ten adults), it brings the mourner into the synagogue in the presence of other mourners and congregants, who can lend support and sympathy and thus help comfort the bereaved.

2. Mourners must sit on hard boxes during shivah to avoid comfort

It is a misconception and erroneous to think that a mourner must sit at home on a hard box during the observance of shivah. Jewish law does not require that mourners sit on boxes. The law merely obligates mourners not to sit on chairs of normal height. This is a way of for the mourners to demonstrated that they have reached a low point in life because of the loss of a loved one. Some explain the custom as a way of expressing the desire to stay close to the earth in which a loved one is now buried. Other scholars base the custom of sitting on low stools on the Bible's description of Job, who, having suffered misfortune, was comforted by friends who sat with him on "the earth."

Sephardic communities do not use stools to the same extent as Ashkenazic Jews. Jews who follow the Moroccan and Judeo-Spanish (Turkish, Greek) tradition often sit directly on the floor, while Syrian Jews sit on the floor but use thin pillows to lessen the discomfort.

Contrary to popular belief, then, Jewish law does not enjoin the bereaved to add discomfort to their grief by sitting on uncomfortable boxes. Losing a loved one is sad enough, and inflicting additional discomfort is antithetical to Jewish thinking.

3. Mourners must wear black when attending a funeral

There is no law requiring a Jew who is bereaved to wear black clothing at the funeral. Nor is there any requirement to wear black clothing during the week of shivah. Perhaps this erroneous idea of the requirement to wear black has as one of its sources the aggadic story that quotes Moses as saying: "Joshua, put on black clothing after my death." When the high priest Simon the Just foretold his impending death, he was asked how he knew. Simon the Just responded, "Every Day of Atonement an old man dressed in white used to escort me as I entered the Holy of Holies. But today I was accompanied by a old man dressed in black."

Although the Bible makes no reference to the wearing of black mourning garments, the Talmud (Shabbat 114a) quotes Rabbi Yannai as having instructed: "Do not bury me in black garments lest I appear without merit." Hence the association of black with death and mourning.

Historically, there were Jews who wore black as a sign that they had lost loved ones. Israel Abrahams, author of *Jewish Life in the Middle Ages*, describes the wearing of black clothing by Jews in Spain, Italy, and Germany. Since they were "Mourners of Zion, the Jews wore the color that was most associated with grief, and that was black."

Although Jewish law does not require black clothing for a mourner, wearing a softened and subdued color seems to be appropriate to the sadness of the occasion.

4. Reincarnation is totally foreign to Jewish thought

A lthough the concept of reincarnation, which asserts that the soul reappears after death in another body, either human or animal, was condemned by most Jewish authorities as heathen superstition, the disciples of Rabbi Isaac Luria, the sixteenth-century kabbalist of Safed, wholeheartedly accepted it as a legitimate Jewish belief. In fact, Rabbi Chayim Vital, the most famous disciple of Rabbi Isaac Luria, wrote a whole book on this theme called *Sefer ha-Gilgulim* ("Book of the Transmigration of Souls").

The belief in the transmigration of souls was an attempt to answer the difficult question of why righteous people suffer while the wicked prosper. The kabbalists believed that if a good person suffered, the good person's soul would migrate to a new body whose life would be one of happiness and prosperity. On the other hand, a sinful and evil person's soul would enter another body that would endure a life of suffering. Over time the belief in transmigration of souls also included the movement of the soul into plants and animals as punishment for especially evil transgressions. Mystics also often use reincarnation to explain odd or unusual occurrences of human characteristics. For example, a kabbalist might conclude that a person who seems to act like an animal is carrying the soul of a beast. According to most mystics, no soul migrates through more than three bodies before it has run its entire course.

According to some, a soul which has sunk to the lowest possible level of contamination becomes an evil spirit in this world and is anxious to enter living bodies to torment them without recourse for punishment in the world-to-come. Such a soul is referred to as a dybbuk. To expel it requires the rites of Jewish exorcism, practiced by kabbalistic wonder-wonders who were influenced by the mystical teachings of Rabbi Isaac Luria.

The similarity between the Jewish belief in reincarnation and that of the Hindu tradition is striking. No one knows for sure whether the Jewish doctrine is a derivation from the Hindu one, but there is scholarly speculation that Jewish mystics became familiar with the idea of reincarnation through the Arabs, who converted many Hindus to Islam. There is also the possibility that Spanish Jews who came into close cultural contact with Muslims during the era of Spain's Golden Age may have learned about the transmigration of souls from them.

Very few modern Jews today accept a belief in reincarnation as basic to their beliefs. Nevertheless it would be imprecise to say that the idea of reincarnation is totally foreign to Jewish thought. It is not!

5. There is no such Jewish belief as resurrection of the dead

People of many faiths believe that in the distant future the dead will be resurrected, coming back to life. In Judaism, according to the dominant rabbinic view, physical resurrection of the dead will take place at the end of time after the arrival of the Messiah. It was Rabbi Elazar HaKappar who taught: "They that are born are destined to die. And the dead are destined to be brought to life again. The living [i.e., the resurrected] are destined after death to be judged" (Ethics of the Fathers 4:28).

There are three and only three biblical texts that announce some form of life after death. Daniel 12:2 was written in the context of the persecutions by Antiochus IV, the villain of the Hanukkah story. It reflects the dilemma of the Jewish pietists who were being martyred precisely because of their loyalty to God. If there is no reward for piety, why die the death of a martyr? The author answers that there is reward for the righteous and punishment for the evildoer, but only after death. "Therefore, many of those that sleep in the dust of the earth will awake, some to eternal life, others to reproaches, to everlasting abhorrence" (Daniel 12:2). The reference here is clearly to bodily resurrection.

Of the two other texts, Isaiah 25:8 and 26:19, the more interesting is Isaiah 25:8: "God will destroy death forever." Not reflected in the Bible itself but central in the later tradition is the Greek notion that humans are composed of a material body which decays and a spiritual soul which never dies. The soul leaves the body at death and enjoys eternal life with God. In time, the two doctrines of bodily resurrection and spiritual immortality were conflated. The body disintegrates at death, the soul remains with God. Then, at the end of days, God unites the body and the soul, and the individual, now reconstituted as in life on earth, comes before God in judgment. This doctrine was central to all of Jewish eschatological thought until the dawn of modernity in the late eighteenth century.

Though most Reform, Conservative, and Reconstructionist Jews have set aside a personal belief in physical resurrection, for more traditionally minded ones, a belief in bodily resurrection continues to radiate great hope. In fact, there is a blessing in some Orthodox prayerbooks that is to be recited when the Messiah comes and all deceased people arise and come back to life!

6. Judaism has no deathbed confessional ritual

The Book of Ecclesiastes (7:2) says, "There is not a righteous person upon earth who does good and does not sin." Whether knowingly or unknowingly, we are all sinners in the course of our lives.

The Torah required that an offering be brought to expiate sins. The Book of Leviticus describes both a sin offering and a guilt offering. With the destruction of the Second Temple in 70 c.e, the sacrificial system was abandoned, and from that time on Jews were deprived of the chance to atone for sins by bringing sacrifices. To fill this void, the ancient rabbis introduced the idea of confession.

The confessional prayer recited on Yom Kippur is fairly well known, and enumerates a litany of sins (many of them sins of the mouth). Many traditional Jews also recite a daily confessional as part of their daily prayers. Individual confessions, however, are made only twice in the lifetime of a Jew—immediately before the marriage ceremony and in the closing moments of one's life.

Jews make confession (*uidduei*) on his or her deathbed, in keeping with the talmudic statement "When a person is sick and near to death, one is asked to make confession" (Talmud, Shabbat 32a). Criminals are urged to confess within a short distance of the scene of execution. If they have nothing to confess, they are instructed to say: "Let my death be an atonement for all of my transgressions" (Talmud, Sanhedrin 6:2).

A gravely ill person is addressed as follows: "Confess your sins. Many confessed their sins and did not die, and many who did not confess died. As a reward for your confession, you will continue to live, for anyone who confesses his sins will have a portion in the world-to-come" (Code of Jewish Law, Yoreh Deah 338:8).

Traditionally, there are two versions of the confessional response recited by the very ill, depending upon the their physical condition. The shorter form is: "May my death be an atonement for all the sins, iniquities, and transgressions of which I have been guilty against You." The confession concludes with the recitation of the Shema: "Hear, O Israel, Adonai is Our God, Adonai is One" (Deuteronomy 6:4).

CHAPTER 6

Ritual Objects and Observances

1. Only a rabbi can perform a funeral or Jewish wedding

The Hebrew word *rabbi* literally means "my teacher." In ancient times, a rabbi was not a credentialed professional hired by a congregation to be its teacher, preacher, and officiant at life-cycle events. Rather, the rabbi was a very learned Jew whom the community engaged as its interpreter and espouser of tradition and Jewish law. In many instances the ancient rabbi was also engaged in another totally unrelated profession (such as a shoemaker) in order to provide sustenance to his family and make an adequate living.

It was probably not until the beginning of the nineteenth century that the profession of rabbi began to consist of formal duties like officiating at life-cycle events such as marriages and funerals and being the emissary of the congregation in prayer.

In bygone years Jewish law did not require involvement by the civil government. Marriage was a private practice between the groom and the bride. A marriage was valid without the presence of a rabbi to substantiate its validity. But the person performing the ceremony was expected to be knowledgeable enough to be certain that the marriage ritual and its procedures were done properly. For according to the Talmud, one who is not versed in the laws of marriage and divorce should not have anything to do with them (Kiddushin 13a). On the other hand, since marriage is not an affair of the state in Jewish law but a private transaction between the bride and groom, the requirement of an officiant was not obligatory. Nonetheless, it was felt that someone versed in the subject of Jewish marriage should supervise the proceedings to ensure compliance with the law. The custom was therefore established that a rabbi or his appointee act as the officiant.

In recent years, especially with the advent of the major schools of Jewish learning in all of the branches of Judaism, beginning in the late nineteenth century, most states enacted laws which required that an ordained rabbi be the officiant of a Jewish marriage ceremony. This also included ordained cantors. In Israel, it is the law of the land that only a duly ordained rabbi, appointed by the chief rabbinate, may officiate at a wedding.

2. Laws of keeping kosher are for reasons of health

Virtually all cultures have rules that regulate eating. Most of Judaism's eating rules are detailed in a tightly organized form in the eleventh chapter of the Book of Leviticus, and they are repeated in modified fashion in the fourteenth chapter of the Book of Deuteronomy. Perhaps one of the most common misconceptions regarding the kosher laws is that it is an ancient health measure which may have had its place in antiquity, but nowadays, with modern methods of slaughter, regular government inspection, and sanitary food preparation, it is quite clearly an anachronism which should be discarded along with the horse and carriage. Neither the Bible nor the Talmud gives any rationale for these laws, and there is no biblical or talmudic evidence that the Jewish dietary laws were enacted for health reasons. There are, however, a number of rationales that do relate to aspects of health.

For example, with regard to fish, the philosopher and scholar Nachmanides differentiates between kosher and non-kosher fish. He posits that kosher fish (i.e., those with fins and scales) are closer to the surface of the water, so they can come up for air, which warms their blood and helps eliminate impurities from their bodies. Fish that do not possess fins and scales do not have this capability.

Maimonides maintains that the reason the pig is forbidden is that it is an offensive animal, feeding on filthy things. Rabbi Shmuel ben Meir posits that all forbidden animals damage the body.

If hygiene and health had been the original reason for the

dietary laws, it could be suggested that with improved health protection and ways of processing food, the dietary laws would no longer be necessary. The most obvious proof that hygiene is not the major reason for the dietary laws is provided by those people who eat prohibited foods and remain healthy. Furthermore, some of the permitted foods can be and have been identified as not particularly advantageous to good health.

The one word that is repeated numerous times in connection with the dietary laws is the word "holy," in Hebrew *kadosh*. By observing the dietary laws, God says, the Israelites will advance in their quest to become a holy people. Jews who keep the dietary laws maintain their distinctiveness as a people. In biblical times, by following a distinctive diet, Israel was encouraged to remain apart, separate from its idol-worshiping neighbors. This lifestyle ensured that the adoption of idolatrous ways by Jews would be kept to a minimum.

3. A yarmulke is a holy object

Wearing a yarmulke (also known as a kippah). is a Jewish custom, not a Jewish law. From talmudic statements it appears that the sages did not walk four steps with uncovered heads (Talmud, Shabbat 118b). In Temple times the priests wore a headdress in the form of a kind of turban while officiating (Exodus 28: 37–39). The Yiddish word *yarmulke* is of uncertain origin, though some think it is a shortened form of two Aramaic words, *yarey me-elohecha* ("one who fears God"). Nowhere in the Torah is a man mandated to cover his head. The head covering has come to symbolize a sign of respect and acknowledgment that there is a God in the universe. In the sixteenth century Rabbi Solomon Luria, one of the leaders of Polish Jewry, was asked by a man who suffered from headaches whether he was permitted to eat without a head covering. Rabbi Luria responded that in theory there was no requirement to wear a head covering even during worship, but, he added, since the custom of Jewish men covering their heads had become widely accepted, people might think that anyone who went about bareheaded was impious. He therefore suggested that the man wear a soft kippah of fine linen or silk.

Because the yarmulke does not have God's name attached to it, it is not considered a holy object in the same way as tefillin, which contain holy parchments with God's name. Unlike tefillin or a prayerbook, which must be buried when they get torn (as are all Jewish holy objects), there is no requirement to do so for a yarmulke.

4. The Star of David is a sacred Jewish symbol that must be displayed in a synagogue

The Star of David, known in Hebrew as *magen david* ("shield of David") has been a symbolic ornament of Judaism for many centuries. It was found in the Capernaum synagogue of the third century C.E. and on a Jewish tombstone in southern Italy. Since the Star of David is not mentioned in rabbinic literature and has been found on Roman mosaic pavements, it is assumed that the star formed of two superimposed triangles is not of Jewish origin.

In 1354, King Charles IV allowed Prague's Jewish community to have its own flag, later known as King David's Flag, upon which there was a six-pointed star. The star became the official emblem of the Jewish community because tradition states that King David himself had a star on his shield.

The first Zionist Congress adopted the star as a symbol, with the word *Tziyyon* (Zion) in the center. During the First World War, it was used as an insignia by Jewish relief organizations.

The Star of David was also used widely in European Jewish communities. As time passed, many synagogues began to use it on their stationery and on walls and stained-glass windows.

Today the Magen David is almost universally recognized as a symbol of Jewry, appearing on the flag of the State of Israel. It is also the symbol of the Israeli counterpart to the Red Cross, known as the Red Magen David.

Although many synagogues today display a Star of David somewhere, there is no religious requirement to do this. The star is simply a symbol of a Jew or Jewish home, and it is a myth to think that it must be prominently placed in a synagogue or temple.

5. All synagogues must display a menorah

The first biblical use of the seven-branched candelabrum is in the Torah, when it was used in the portable sanctuary known as the Tabernacle, set up by Moses in the wilderness (Exodus 27:21). It also was a permanent fixture in both the first and second Temples in Jerusalem. In both Temples the candelabrum was provided daily with fresh olive oil of the purest quality and burned from morning to evening. After the Temples were destroyed, a tradition developed that the appurtenances of the Temple should not be duplicated and that seven-branched menorahs should not be constructed (Talmud, Menachot 28b). The six-branched menorah became popular, but any number other than seven was permissible. A Star of David was usually affixed to the center arm of the six-branched menorah.

There is no Jewish law today that requires a synagogue to have a seven-branched menorah in its sanctuary. Those congregations that have them reason that they are not copies of the candelabrum of the Temple. Since modern menorahs are electrified, they are quite unlike the original, which had to be cleaned each day and provided with new wicks and fresh oil.

6. If you drop a Torah scroll the penalty is fasting for forty days.

The Code of Jewish Law (Orach Chayim 3:3) states that a person who drops a Torah scroll is required to fast. Some say the fast is to last for forty days. In addition, those who see the scroll fall are also required to fast. The forty-day fast does not have to be forty days in a row and only includes the daylight hours, not the night before. The idea here is that the Torah is a holy object, and to drop it indicates a certain lack of care and recognition of its sanctity. And when someone does something wrong, certain acts, such as fasting, can lessen that person's accountability. Fasting atones for the disrespect shown to the Torah.

The biggest risk of dropping a Torah scroll occurs when someone is given the honor of lifting the scroll (*hagba*). This is especially true on Simchat Torah, when the worshipers are generally ecstatic and dancing wildly while holding the Torah scroll high above their heads. It has been facetiously said that the trick in not worrying about dropping the scroll is "to eat the night before."

These days people are not as hardy as they used to be Instead of declaring a fast, the alternative custom is making a tzedakah contribution to a worthy cause. The act of making a charitable donation as a result of dropping a Torah scroll seems much more beneficial to humanity than the act of personal fasting.

7. Jewish boys must have a Bar Mitzvah in order to be considered for Jewish manhood

A Bar Mitzvah (or Bat Mitzvah for girls) is one of the important life-cycle events in the life of any Jewish child. Joseph Telushkin, in his book *Jewish Literacy* (p. 611), has the following test of Jewish knowledge: "Fill in the blank. The one religious ceremony that a boy must perform at thirteen in order to become Bar Mitzvah is _____. The correct answer is none."

A boy becomes a Bar Mitzvah by virtue of reaching the age of thirteen, and is considered a Bar Mitzvah (i.e., obligated to perform religious commandments) whether or not he has an actual Bar Mitzvah ceremony in a synagogue. Thus, whether a boy (or a girl) participates in a special religious service or not, the status of Bar or Bat Mitzvah is automatic, conferred upon them by virtue of their chronological age. The words *bar mitzvah* literally mean "son of the commandments." According to Jewish law, at age thirteen and girls (in nonorthodox denominations) according to one's Hebrew birthday, a Jewish child is bound by the commandments. In Judaism boys become obligated to fulfill Jewish laws at thirteen, while for girls the age is twelve in orthodox Judaism, since girls tend to mature earlier. Jewish law recognized the age of thirteen as the beginning of a boy's physical maturity and a stage in which a young man could begin to exercise control of his emotions and desires. In Jewish legendary literature, the age of thirteen was the turning in the life of Judaism's first patriarch, Abraham, when he rejected the idol worship of his father, Terach.

Becoming a Bar Mitzvah in North America today generally

entails attending a Jewish religious school and learning life-cycle events, Jewish history, Hebrew language, and Jewish customs and ceremonies. In addition, many Bar Mitzvah and Bat Mitzvah students also read from the Torah in the synagogue or temple on the day of their Bar/Bat Mitzvah and may also chant a Haftarah (a prophetic portion from one of the books of the Prophets).

It is a misconception to think that there is such a verb as "barmitzvahed," as in a person saying "I was barmitzvahed by Rabbi So-and-So at Temple Beth El." In Judaism one *becomes* a Bar Mitzvah on attaining the appropriate age; another person's actions cannot confer the status of Bar Mitzvah.

8. Judaism has no interest in seeking converts

There is a widespread myth that Judaism has no interest in seeking converts. In actuality, Jews in bygone centuries actively sought converts. In the Talmud (Pesachim 87a), it is related that Rabbi Eleazar ben Pedat declared that God sent the Jews into exile to bring people to Judaism. Writing in the first century of the common era, the famous Jewish historian Josephus reported that women were more apt than men to become Jews, probably because there was no necessity for them to undergo the painful event of circumcision.

The pace of conversion was greatly curtailed as a result of the defeat of the Jews by the Romans in the first and second centuries. The spread of Christianity throughout the Roman Empire also greatly limited the pace of conversions. Still, in the fourth century of the common era, after the Roman Empire became Christian, it was a crime to convert to Judaism, indicating that conversions were indeed still taking place. In the Arab world, Muslim religious leaders also made conversion to Judaism a capital crime.

By the Middle Ages, the Jewish community was actively discouraging conversion, believing that the danger in the conversion process was much too risky. As late as the eighteenth century, Count Valentine Potocki, a convert to Judaism, was burned at the stake in Vilna.

Today, a good many conversions occur in connection with the marriage of an interfaith couple. Although marriage is not the ideal motive for conversion, most rabbis will support the prospective convert if they believe that the convert intends to live a committed Jewish life.

It is estimated that many thousands of people convert to Judaism each year in the United States.

9. A male child is not a Jew until he is circumcised

The oldest ritual in Judaism is that of circumcision (in Hebrew *brit milah*). This ceremony dates back to the time of the patriarch Abraham, who at age ninety-nine was instructed by God to have himself circumcised (Genesis 17:9–14). Later, Abraham was charged by God to circumcise his son Isaac on the eighth day, as an outward sign of God's covenant.

It is a bubbe meise to think that circumcision makes a person Jewish, for he is Jewish already by birth. The circumcision testifies that he who bears this sign sealed in his flesh is under the covenant, which is what gives meaning to life. Through the covenant he is bound to all other Israelites and through them to God.

Jewish law indicates specifically that circumcision is to take place on the eighth day, unless there are medical problems related to the baby's health. If perchance a baby is medically circumcised but the proper blessings are not recited or the circumcision did not take place on the prescribed eighth day, then a symbolic circumcision, known as a *hatafat dam brit* (spilling of a drop of blood) takes place. This ceremony, which involves a pinprick on the male genital that lets out a spot of blood, must be done by a *mohel* or a qualified Jewish physician. The *hatafat dam brit* ceremony is also used for a non-Jewish adult male (who has been surgically circumcised) who converts to Judaism.

10. A Jewish child must be named after a deceased relative

Naming a child has always been a significant experience. In the case of Jewish names, there is the added significance of Jewish identity. The rabbis of old said that one of the reasons why God redeemed the children of Israel from Egyptian bondage was that they had retained their Jewish names (Midrash, Leviticus Rabbah 32:5). It is customary to name a male child at the circumcision and a female child in the synagogue. The naming of boys is part of the circumcision ceremony. Girl babies are often named in the synagogue during a worship service.

Aside from this, there are no legal requirements regarding the naming of a Jewish child, but there are customs which vary depending on geographic location. So, for example, amongst Ashkenazic Jews (those originally from Central and Eastern Europe), the custom is to honor the departed by naming a child after someone who is deceased. However, among Sephardic Jews (those originating from Middle Eastern countries), the custom is the polar opposite. Sephardim name after the living.

We are not certain as to why these two groups of Jewish people took opposite paths. Some have surmised that Ashkenazic Jews associate the name with a person's soul, and that to name a child after a living person would somehow or other shorten the life span of that person. In addition, to have several people in a family named after the same person might lead to some confusion.

Among Hasidic Jews the custom is often to name children after the tzaddik to whom the family is devoted. Today some families have substituted the names of civic or moral leaders.

CHAPTER

Jewish Superstitions

1. There are benefits to chewing on thread

Chewing on thread is a delightfully superstitious bubbe meise that is still often practiced today by dedicated Jewish old-timers who value the custom. The custom is to chew on a piece of thread when wearing a garment upon which someone is actively sewing. Whether it be repairing a seam, sewing a button, or repairing a tear, if you are wearing the clothing and someone is going to be sewing it, the custom is to chew on the thread.

Two reasons have been posited for this strange custom. While Jews, as a group at least, have never been believers in shrunken heads, one explanation is suggested by the Yiddish phrase *mir zollen nit farnayen der saychel*—"we should not sew up the brains [or common sense]." A second reason put forth is that the remains of the deceased are sewn into their burial shrouds, known as *tachrichin*. As an avoidance of this, we don't sew on garments we are wearing. Active chewing, conceivably, may show that the person wearing the garment is not deceased but is still with us.

2. Saying "pooh pooh pooh" at the right time has real value

S aying "pooh pooh pooh" was one of my mother's favorite expressions when I was a child. The saying is authoritatively captured in the well-known film *Fiddler on the Roof.*

"Pooh pooh pooh" was an old wives' tale and custom, evolved as a refined expectoration based on the practice of spitting after one witnessed a terrible sight, heard a bad tale, and the like. It was also done when witnessing or remarking upon something exceptionally good or wonderful, such as seeing a beautiful, healthy child, hearing of a recent engagement, or discussing other good news. It was done so that the evil would not happen or befall us again.

The reason for the spitting is that saliva was long considered a potent anti-demonic safeguard. Jews believed that demons and playful spirits abounded everywhere and were forever ready to do evil or mischief. And thus the bubbe meise arose that spitting brought positive results.

Ancients and medieval thinkers wrote about the value of spittle and saliva. Even the medieval physician Maimonides speaks favorably about the positive use of saliva.

The phrase "pooh pooh pooh" was also considered an antidote to the so-called evil eye. Spitting three times on one's fingertips (evil spirits had a propensity for alighting there) and each time making a quick movement with one's hand in the air was expected to do the trick in eradicating them.

3. Never leave home for a trip without taking tzedakah

A common practice in the past and still current today is to give someone who is about to take a trip some money to be given away as charity upon arrival at his or her destination. The money itself is often called *mitzvah gelt*, "good deed money," and the person making the journey is known in Hebrew as a *shaliach mitzvah*, meaning "messenger of a good deed."

The practice of giving mitzvah gelt is probably predicated upon the talmudic principle that "agents of a mitzvah are not harmed" (Pesachim 8a). In other words, the Talmud maintains that a person who is on the way to perform a mitzvah is protected. Therefore, giving a traveler a bit of cash to be given to a pauper at the destination makes the traveler an agent for the delivery of this *tzedakah* money and thereby protected. The transformation of a person who is traveling for mundane, non-religious reasons into a messenger of a good deed brings the traveler under the sanction of divine guardianship to complete this specific act.

4. Pick up your ears when you sneeze

There is a great old bubbe meise that, if practiced, makes people look at you every time you sneeze to see how you are going to inconspicuously move your hands up to your hears to pull them. This bubbe meise custom seems to have enjoyed greater popularity among Jews from Galicia and Lithuania. Arguments arise as to whether one ear will suffice or both are necessary, and whether the ears are to be gently pulled or to be tugged.

The exact reason for the picking up of the ears in unclear. The ear pulling was supposed to be done if the sneeze occurred during a conversation about someone who was deceased. In some circles, it is applied to sneezing in general, and is accompanied by reciting the Yiddish phrase *Tzu layngeh mazaldikker yohrn*—"To long, lucky years."

5. Thou shalt not count Jews

A long-standing bubbe meise relates to counting Jewish people. As crazy as this sounds, there are still plenty of traditional Jews who simply will not count Jews. There are a variety of reasons for this rather unusual custom.

The Torah itself first hints at the problem of counting Jews when it says: "When you take the sum of the children of Israel according to their counting, then each man will give atonements for his soul when you count them; then there will be no plague as you count them" (Exodus 30:12).

In the Bible, counting is connected with the occurrence or avoidance of plagues. It is mentioned in both Exodus and II Samuel. A second reason is that King David's census taking was for a war of aggression, so that he would know how many able-bodied men he would have, and this is considered an act alien to the spirit of Judaism. Following King David's census, the plague of pestilence did indeed occur, taking some seventy thousand lives.

In the realm of superstition, some considered the prohibition of counting people to be a way of foiling the Angel of Death, either so that he would not know how many Jews there are or would not feel egged on to do his job even more efficiently.

Not counting Jews also applies to determining whether there are enough people present at a worship service for prayer—in other words, a minyan of ten adults. Here, instead of counting heads, some follow the custom of reciting a ten-word liturgical phrase or song, each word corresponding to one of the people in the room. If you don't have a minyan, you can't complete the phrase. A popular Hebrew verse for this purpose is Psalm 28:9: "Deliver and bless Your own peo-ple, tending and sustaining them." By saying the words rather than counting by number, one fulfills the "commandment" of "Thou shalt not count Jews." The idea here is that each human being is unique, and a person's qualities cannot be reduced to some numerical quantity.

6. Safety-pins—never leave home without them

The rationale for wearing a pin or carrying one in my pocket eluded me for years. My maternal grandmother always carried one, and would often say in her Galician Yiddish that *barzel maynt mazal*—"iron means luck." *Barzel* is also the acronym for the names of Jacob's wives, the founding mothers of the Twelve Tribes of Israel: Bilhah, Rachel, Zilpah, and Leah. In a vast overview of their lives, they too averted all dangers.

In the realm of Jewish superstition, metals were believed to have protective power. As the products of civilization, they were antagonistic to the spirit masters of pre-metal society, according to Rabbi Eleazar of Worms in the twelfth century. Metal is obviously protective, as can be concluded from Exodus 7:19, in which God says of the first plague that all water stored "in vessels of wood and vessels of stone" will turn to blood. Since metal receptacles are not mentioned, it is presumed that they protect the water within from turning to blood. Either which way, metal was purported to have a strongly protective nature. Wearing or carrying a small protective item of metal like a pin was only to hedge one's bets for safety, for there is no official Jewish requirement to do so.

7. Chicken soup has no therapeutic value

The notion that eating chicken soup when one is ill has medicinal value is often dismissed as a Jewish old wives' tale. For years, Jews have served chicken soup not only as a Shabbat staple, but also when people have colds, fevers, and even pneumonia. Amazingly, the American Medical Association (in real laboratory studies) has confirmed the therapeutic value of eating chicken soup. Chicken soup has long been recognized as possessing potency against a wide variety of viral and bacterial agents. And as early as the twelfth century, the philosopher and physician Moses Maimonides wrote that chicken is recommended as an excellent food as well as a medication.

8. There is no such thing as Jewish astrology

It is surely false to assume that Judaism does not support an astrological system. Astrology is the study of the positions and relationships of the sun, moon, planets, and stars in order to judge their influence on human actions. Unlike astronomy, astrology is not a scientific study and has often been criticized by scientists. However, it clearly continues to be part of the belief system of many people, judging by the popularity of horoscopes and fortune-telling along with the many books on the subject.

There can be no doubt that Jews in ancient times did believe in astrology. Many talmudic scholars are quoted as believing in it, although some of them posited that the stars had no influence over Jews, who were under direct divine influence.

In the Babylonian Talmud, astrologers are known as *kaldiyyim* (Pesachim 113b). The Jerusalem Talmud more frequently uses the term *astrologia* for "astrology."

Many talmudic rabbis believed that the heavenly bodies played a major role in determining human affairs in the sublunar world. In one instance, Abraham and his progeny are spoken of as having been elevated beyond subjection to the stars (Midrash, Genesis Rabbah 44:12). Several instances are cited in the Talmud of astrologers whose predictions of future events came true. For example, in Shabbat 119, a man named Joseph who was always honored for observing the Sabbath was told by an astrologer that he would consume all of the property of a certain gentile. When the gentile learned of this, he sold all his property and bought a precious jewel with the proceeds, which he placed in his turban for safekeeping. As he was crossing a bridge, a wind blew the turban into the water. A fish swallowed the turban, and subsequently Joseph caught the fish and brought it to market on the eve of the Sabbath. When Joseph opened the fish, he discovered the jewel, and thus the astrologer's prediction came true!

Traces of the ancient Jewish belief in the stars influencing people can be found in some of the words used by ancient rabbis and still used today. For example, the popular phrase *mazal tov*, which is often interpreted as meaning "good fortune" or "good luck," literally refers to "a good star."

The *Shulchan Aruch*, Judaism's most authoritative law code, states categorically that "one should not consult astrologers, nor should one cast lots in order to determine the future" (Yoreh Deah 179:1).

There are many vestiges of astrology in Jewish folklore. For example, one should not start any business on the new moon, on Friday (*Sifra*, Kedoshim 6). Also, it dangerous to drink water on Wednesday and Friday evenings (Talmud, Pesachim 112a). One should perform marriages only in the first half of the month while the moon is waxing (Nachmanides, responsum 282). And finally, an unslept-in bed (called the bed of Gad) in a house is a good luck charm (Talmud, Moed Katan 27a).

9. There is no such thing as biblical magic verses

The prohibition of magic that one finds in the Bible also finds expression in the Talmud. For instance, Sanhedrin 7:7 equates magic with idolatry. And in tractate Sotah 48a it states that harlotry and magic cause mass destruction. This being said, there are biblical verses that nonetheless were used for magical purposes. These are usually verses that include God's name or refer to God's power. The Book of Psalms was considered an especially potent book for magical purposes. Perhaps the most popular book on the subject of magic using psalms is the *Shimmush Tehillim* ("Use of Psalms"). This book was written in the mid-1500s, and its opening line states that "the entire Torah is composed of the names of God, and in consequence it has the property of saving and protecting man." The book quotes a tradition that when a town or city is endangered, it can be saved by reciting in order those psalms whose initial letters spell out the name of the city.

Another work, the *Sefer Gematriot*, lists a series of biblical verses and their magical use. Although some of these verses were recited exactly as found in the Bible, others were recited by reversing the usual order, transposing words, or repeating them a given number of times. Sometimes the words were dissolved in a liquid and drunk, or worn as an amulet. Here are some magical verses from the *Sefer Gematriot*:

1. For a child who has been recently circumcised: "So he blessed them that day saying, By you shall Israel invoke blessings, saying: God make you like Ephraim and Manasseh" (Genesis 48:20).

2. To drive off evil spirits, recite before going to sleep: "God bless you and protect you. May God deal kindly and graciously with you. May God bestow favor on you and grant you peace" (Numbers 6:24–26).

3. To gain a good name: "You are fair, my darling, you are fair, with your dove-like eyes" (Song of Songs 6:4–9).

4. For a melodious voice: "Then Moses and the Israelites sang this song to God. They said: I will sing to God, for God has triumphed gloriously. Horse and driver God has thrown into the sea" (Exodus 15:1).

5. To arouse love: "Your ointments yield a sweet fragrance, your name is like finest oil. Therefore do maidens love you" (Song of Songs 1:3).

6. For a fever: "So Moses cried to God, saying: O God, pray heal her" (Numbers 12:13).

CHAPTER  8

Sex

1. The offspring of an unmarried couple is regarded as illegitimate

Judaism has always maintained and valued the importance of sexual intimacy in the context of marriage. Adam and Eve, the progenitors of all humanity, according to the biblical story, were specifically created for each other, "for it is not good that a person be alone, and therefore a man leaves his father and his mother and clings to his wife, so that they become one flesh" (Genesis 2:18, 24). The Torah thus recognizes the basic human need for intimate companionship and seeks to satisfy that need through the institution of marriage. Sex within marriage continues to be the ideal. Although the Torah never explicitly outlaws non-marital sex (except in the case of adultery and incest), the rabbis forbade it. Sex outside marriage simply did not fit their ideal of holiness and could lead to continued promiscuity after marriage.

Judaism and its spokespersons do not very often refer to an unmarried couple living together as living in sin. Furthermore, Jewish law has never regarded a sexual relationship between an unmarried couple with the same stringency as it does an adulterous relationship between married people. Nor is a child born out of wedlock in Judaism considered a mamzer. In Jewish law, only a child born of a forbidden relationship (e.g., a brother marrying his sister) is considered a mamzer. Today a child born out of wedlock is not stigmatized in the same way as the offspring of an adulterous relationship.

In order to discourage intimacy among engaged couples a change was made in the marriage ritual. In bygone years two separate ceremonies occurred several months apart. First there was betrothal, and then there was marriage, allowing for the husband and wife to live together under one roof. The ancient rabbis, concerned about the problem of sexual intimacy between the time of the betrothal ceremony and the marriage ceremony, decided eventually to combine the two ceremonies into one. This is the law today.

2. Jewish law is totally opposed to birth control

I n truth, Judaism is relatively permissive with regard to artificial contraception on the woman's part. This is because
she is technically not commanded to procreate (although
when she marries she joins with her husband in the fulfillment of this mitzvah). Second, her use of birth control does
not involve the serious transgression of destroying seed.

As in so many other cases, religious authorities differ on
which purposes and methods of contraception they will permit. The most lenient authorities would say that birth control
is permissible as long as normal intercourse can take place
and one body derives natural gratification from the other. For
these more liberal rabbinic authorities, the diaphragm and
the contraceptive patch are the most favored forms of birth
control, for they prevent contraception and have little if any
impact on the woman's health. If the contraceptive pill or
implant is not contraindicated by a woman's age or body
chemistry, it is usually the form of contraception that these
liberal rabbinic authorities most favor. They recommend
these methods because their success rate minimizes the possibility of the couple later considering an abortion as a form of
retroactive birth control. Orthodox rabbinic authorities posit
that contraceptive devices may never be used by the male and
even the female may resort to them only on pressing medical
grounds.

Because rabbinic law enjoins that only a man is commanded to be fruitful and multiply (Genesis 1:28), Judaism is
more restrictive about condoms, whose use violates the strict
prohibition against the wasting of seed. The severe rabbinic
stricture on the wasting of seed was related to the belief that

the male seed was really a person in miniature waiting to be planted in female soil and that the number of seeds was limited. Because we now know that this is not true, many rabbinic authorities permit the use of condoms. In addition, because condoms are known to protect not only against pregnancy but against sexually transmitted diseases, particularly AIDS, there is a stronger push for their use.

3. Judaism advocates sex for purposes of procreation only

" God blessed Adam and Eve and said: Be fruitful and multiply" (Genesis 1:28). This is the first of the Torah's 613 commandments, and clearly indicates the duty to have children as a mitzvah. However, Judaism also advocates that sex is a lofty pursuit, and that having a fulfilled sex life is essential to a healthy marriage. The Zohar, the book of Jewish mysticism, added that the Sabbath candles are a symbol of a wife's ability to rekindle her husband's lust and passion for her. Just as the Shabbat candles flicker with great intensity and burning, always renewing themselves after a flicker and momentary dimming of their flames, so, too, a woman can always renew her husband's interest in her even after a hiatus of passion and excitement.

God wishes for husbands and wives to be happy together. "Had sexual relations been only physical," the medieval rabbi Menachem Meiri argued, "the Bible would not have referred to them as *yediah* (knowledge)." The great Bible commentator Rashi furthermore writes that the true connection between husband and wife cannot be achieved without pleasure: "since if she does not enjoy intimacy, she will not cleave to him." This type of mutually satisfying bond is achieved with pleasure as the central ingredient of lovemaking.

4. Traditional Jews mandate a hole in the sheet when making love

It is a misconception to think that Jews must make love with the use of a sheet. The truth of the matter is not only that Jewish law does not mandate the use of a sheet, but that it would not allow it if the couple desired one out of some ill-conceived sense of piety. The rabbis of old did not allow any articles of clothing to be worn during lovemaking. And a couple is permitted to don anything they want during foreplay to arouse each other. Judaism's constant position when it comes to lovemaking is that God is omnipresent and a factor in all relationships, and therefore arousal techniques should be in consonance with the holiness of the act. The ancient rabbis did, however, strongly advocate that lovemaking take place in the dark, since the dark requires a couple to see with the eye of their minds, and fantasy and mystery are more easily integrated into the experience. Rabbinic consensus also holds that sex should take place well into the evening, a time when husband and wife are more relaxed and released from the cares of the world. The Talmud adds that it is a special mitzvah for a scholar to have intercourse on Friday night, thus joining the holiness of the Sabbath with the holiness of marital sex—a double mitzvah!

5. Masturbation is strictly forbidden in Judaism

The answer to the question "Is it proper in Judaism to masturbate?" depends on whom you ask. Traditional Judaism generally forbids masturbation by males and has little to say about masturbation by females.

Modern rabbinic views vary on the subject of permissibility. For instance, the Orthodox Rabbi Reuven P. Bulka, in his book *Judaism on Pleasure*, strongly condemns masturbation because in his view it is an instrument for focusing only on oneself. Rabbi Elliot Dorff, a Conservative rabbi, in his book *Matters of Life and Death*, writes that masturbation in and of itself should no longer carry the shame it had for our ancestors: the original grounds for opposing it (that a man has a finite amount of seed and spilling saps a man's strength) are no longer tenable, and it is a way of dealing with one's sexual energy before marriage. Others agree with him, positing that learning about one's body is permissible. Therefore, they have declared masturbation a permissible form of release, because it can work to discourage young people from sexual experimentation with others.

Rabbi Shmuley Boteach, in his book *Kosher Sex*, writes that every act of masturbation serves as a powerful release that in turn lessens our vital need for sex with another person. In the context of marriage, the lessening of need for sex can be disastrous.

6. Fantasizing about another woman while making love is forbidden

The rabbis differ as to whether it is permissible for a man to fantasize about another woman when he has sex with his wife: "so that you do not follow your heart and eyes in your lustful urge" (Numbers 15:39). Deducing from this, Rabbi Judah the Prince taught: "One may not drink out of one goblet and think about another." Rabina said: This is necessary only when both are his wives" (Talmud, Nedarim 20b). Rabina's opinion permits sexual fantasies about another woman not available in the household. Such fantasies would not threaten a woman's status in her own household as would a fantasy about a co-wife.

In our own times, some Jewish sources would permit a man to fantasize about a beautiful but unavailable movie star it if helps intensify lovemaking with his own wife. However, a fantasy that might lead to infidelity (e.g., one about a neighbor's wife). would be inappropriate and not permissible.

7. Jewish sources are unforgiving when it comes to adultery

According to an old joke often told by rabbis, Moses comes down from the mountain carrying the two tablets and says, "I have good news and bad news. The good news is, I got Him down to ten. The bad news is, adultery is still out."

Adultery is as old as the human race. An ancient midrash says that Cain killed Abel because they were fighting over who would sleep with Eve, their mother and Adam's wife. Basic to Judaism is the sanctity of marriage and the importance of fidelity. If the ideal is that "a man leaves his father and mother and clings to his wife" (Genesis 2:24), then to cling to another on the side goes against God's plan for humanity.

Adultery is the only sexual transgression mentioned in the Ten Commandments. The Torah makes it a capital crime for both the woman who commits adultery and her lover, and it is one of three transgressions for which it is better to die than to transgress. The Ten Commandments even outlaw coveting another man's wife. In the Torah, if a man suspected his wife of committing adultery, he could put her through a trial by ordeal in which she was forced to drink bitter waters. If she was guilty, she was convicted by manifesting certain physical symptoms (Numbers 5:11–31). The rabbis were quite uncomfortable with this trial by ordeal. The Mishnah teaches "When adulterers increased in number, the application of the waters of jealousy ceased. And Rabbi Yochanan ben Zakkai abolished them" (Sotah 9:9).

In biblical times the punishment for proven adultery was

death. But to make it virtually impossible ever to put someone to death, the rabbis placed numerous restrictions on the possibility of conviction. For example, they required two witnesses to the adulterous act, proper warning, and acknowledgment of the warning. By talmudic times, lashes were substituted for capital punishment.

The Torah prohibits the woman who commits adultery from returning to her husband. The rabbis also forbade her to her lover, and if she married her lover, the rabbis could force them to divorce.

But in spite of this, there is ample precedent in Jewish sources for a more forgiving attitude to the adulterer. God tells the prophet Hosea to take a wife with a reputation for harlotry. Hosea marries Gomer and has several children, but she commits adultery. Yet in the end Hosea takes her back. The idea here is that Hosea came to understand that his relationship with his wife symbolized the relationship between God and the people Israel. Israel was the wife who played the harlot by worshiping idols. In the end, though, God would take Israel back.

CHAPTER 9

Opinions about Jews

1. Jews are smarter than people of other faiths

There is no biological or statistic evidence that Jews are smarter than anyone else. However, there is no question that Jews do seem to have a reputation for being smart. This reputation is likely a result of the emphasis that Jews place on the value of education.

Giving a Jewish child an education has always been considered one of the most important religious obligations of a parent. The ideal education in Judaism is achieved when both the home and the school prepare the child to take his or her place in the world. Two thousand years ago, before there were synagogue schools, parents were the primary teachers of their children. When schools began to emerge, parents and schoolteachers shared the role of educating children.

The importance placed on the value of an education has continued to the present day, as Jewish parents continue to look to send their children to the finest schools and encourage them to attain a college education. Consequently, as a result of all of this education, Jews in our country continue to be high achievers. Although the Jewish people are but a small minority, we have produced an extraordinary large number of Nobel Prize winners in many subject areas. In fact, statistics show that Jews constitute 36 percent of all U.S. Nobel Prize winners. Such amazing statistics surely foster the reputation of Jewish culture and religion as placing a high value on education, and reinforce the belief that Jews are in fact smarter than other people.

2. Jews are tight with money

It is a bubbe meise to believe that Jews are tight with money. Some of the greatest philanthropists in the world are Jews who have given millions of dollars to a variety of charities. Ordinary Jews, too, are also noted for their charitable giving. That being said, it is true that there seems to be a perception among some people that Jews have a reputation for being tight with their money.

During the Middle Ages, Jews began to specialize in banking and money lending. The banking profession was one of the few professions open to Jews in an antisemitic society when many professions were prohibited to them. For centuries, there had been no real need for money. Things not grown by a landowner on his own soil, and not manufactured by serfs or slaves, were obtained by barter. Extra money needed for building churches or castles or for waging wars used to be borrowed, at some interest, from wealthy monasteries.

When European life became more settled in the Middle Ages, human wants increased and merchants needed capital. Many Jews lent the wealth they had accumulated during years of mercantile activity to princes or Christian merchants. Even some churches and cathedrals were erected with money borrowed from Jews.

It so happened that about this time the Catholic Church began to proclaim the theory that any interest, no matter how small, was usury. It announced that a Christian dared not lend money to another Christian in the hope of gain. If he did so, he was guilty of a great sin and deserved to be excommunicated.

William Shakespeare has been accused of antisemitism for creating the character of Shylock the moneylender. Appearing in the play *The Merchant of Venice*, Shylock is a Jewish moneylender who insists that a non-Jew, Antonio, repay his overdue loan with a pound of flesh drawn from near his heart. Shylock is prevented by a legal trick from accomplishing this goal, but the damage inflicted on the Jews by this story continues to this day. Surprisingly, Shakespeare never met or even saw a Jew, since the Jews were expelled from England in 1290, more than three hundred and fifty years before his birth, and were not readmitted until 1656, forty years after his death.

The image of Jews as a nation of moneylending Shylocks persisted throughout the Middle Ages into modern times. To this day, the illegal industry of high-interest loans is known as "shylocking."

When Charles Dickens fashioned another stereotypical Jewish villain called Fagin, who made his living training young boys to become pickpockets, the reputation of Jews vis-à-vis money became even more exaggerated.

3. A Jew can believe in Jesus and still be Jewish

Judaism cannot be detached from belief in or beliefs about God. Residing always at the very heart of our self-understanding as a people, and of all Jewish culture and literature, God permeates our language, our law, our conscience, and our lore.

All of the major Jewish denominations affirm the critical importance of belief in an incorporeal God, but they do not specify all the particulars of that belief. However, belief in a Trinitarian God or in Jesus as the Son of God can never be consistent with Jewish tradition and history.

To Christians, Jesus is the Son of God and the Messiah. If one carefully reviews Jesus's attitude to Judaism and its laws and way of life, it would become quite apparent that Jesus would not qualify as a prophet or as a rabbi in the religious sense, let alone be the Son of God. In all important respects, Jesus placed himself in opposition to the faith into which he was born. He also broke with a long and clearly established biblical tradition that no human being can ever be divine.

Since according to the Jewish legal definition a Jew is anyone born of a Jewish mother, a Jew who believes in Jesus would still technically qualify as Jewish. However, such a Jew would be considered an apostate, a Jewish defector. Essentially, this means that a member, for example, of a group such as Jews for Jesus or any other Hebrew-Christian missionary movement would be rejected for membership in a synagogue.

4. Hasidism is a cult

S ome people have noticed similarities between cult leaders and the spiritual leaders of Hasidism, a Jewish religious movement. Each Hasidic sect is led by a charismatic central authority known as its rebbe, and its members are beholden to him for all kinds of practical advice. There are some differences, though. In a cult there is blind obedience to the leader, and all assets belong to the cult. In addition, a cult requires its members to break their family ties. The new community becomes a substitute family. In addition, a cult views itself as the only true religion, and anyone who disagrees with the group is viewed as an agent of the devil.

There members of any Hasidic group have personal autonomy, although their spiritual and religious customs tend to be similar. The family in a Hasidic sect is not required to give its earnings to the rebbe. Certainly, members of any Hasidic group are allowed to think for themselves, although the rebbe is generally the final authority. Therefore, it would be a gross misrepresentation to think that a Hasidic sect is tantamount to a cult.

5. Synagogue services are only open to Jews

There is a misconception and rather common notion among non-Jews that the synagogue is a place of mystery, inaccessible to those outside of the Jewish faith. Such a belief is totally unwarranted. Any person may enter a synagogue at any time. Often inscribed on the walls of synagogues are the words of the prophet Isaiah: "My house shall be a house of worship of all peoples."

It is true that if a non-Jew visits a synagogue and is a male, he may be asked to cover his head with a yarmulke that will be provided by one of the ushers. This is because the covering of one's head is seen as a sign of respect and reverence for God. Non-Jews may also, if they choose, join in on the prayers. There are prayers in the Jewish worship service that replicate those that might be said in a church, including the universalistic Psalm 145, which ends with the words "We will praise You from this time forth and forevermore, Halleluyah."

In recent years, many synagogues have welcomed visitors from other faiths who have chosen to visit during a worship group in order to learn more about the Jewish religion. The visitors will often be invited to stay after the service so that a knowledgeable member of the congregation can offer a tour of the building and answer questions Christians may have about synagogue ritual and the things they see in the synagogue sanctuary. Invariably visitors have found synagogues most willing to explain the various symbols, thus contributing to their appreciation and understanding of Judaism as the wellspring of Christianity. Some synagogues offer adult education courses and encourage people of other faiths to attend.

Nobody, whatever his or her faith, need hesitate about entering a synagogue, whether it be to observe, study, meditate, or even pray.

6. Women are second-class citizens in Judaism

One of the most sexist sit-com characters ever to appear on television was Archie Bunker, in the TV hit *All in the Family*. In one episode, to prove his point that men are superior to women, Archie quotes one of the Jewish morning blessings: "Thank God I am not a woman."

At first blush, this blessing certainly seems to imply male superiority over women. But in looking more closely at the blessing in the context in which it was written, the blessing is a prayer that praises God for affording men the privilege of performing all religious rites. Women do not have such a requirement, because, according to Jewish law, women were given an exemption from most religious duties that have to be carried out at a fixed time. Since women in bygone years were so fully occupied with their domestic duties, it was next to impossible for them to become involved in the social and religious affairs of the community. For this reason, they were excused from rituals having a specific time of performance. Their responsibilities to children and family needed to take priority.

Thus the blessing "who has not made me a woman" was in no way intended to remind Jews of the second-class citizenship of women. The enlightened attitude of the Jewish sages to women is best reflected in such statements as "The Holy Blessed One gave a greater measure of understanding to woman than to man" (Talmud, Niddah 45b) and "A man, to know peace in his home, should honor his wife even more than himself" (Talmud, Yevamot 62b). Throughout history, the status of the Jewish woman, though more limited than that of the Jewish man, was historically always higher and more privileged than that of her non-Jewish counterpart.

In the Western world over time, the social and communal role of Jewish women rose to greater and greater equality. In religious matters, however, change has been slower, although today in the non-Orthodox synagogue world there are many females serving congregations both as rabbis and cantors. Women in the non-Orthodox world are for the most part given full religious equality.

7. Orthodox men don't shake hands with a woman

Orthodox Jews believe in the separation of the sexes in a variety of ways. These practices are reflected in the fact that during Temple times there was a special women's court, and men and women were separated. Women occupied their special separate section to avoid any possible frivolity resulting from contact with men. Today, in Orthodox synagogues, men and women continue to sit separately during prayer services.

There is a concept in Judaism called *siyag la-Torah*, "safeguarding the Torah." Essentially this concept holds that there are times when, although something is theoretically permissible according to Jewish law, one ought to refrain from doing it because it might lead to a violation of the law. An Orthodox man not shaking hands with a woman might well fall into the category of safeguarding, and has nothing to do with rudeness. The fear, here, is that by touching the hand of a woman, there is always the possibility of becoming sexually aroused or interested romantically in that woman. Since in Orthodox Judaism a man is permitted to have sexual relations only with his wife, the fear would be that even touching the hand of a woman (other than his own wife) could lead to temptation.

Because there are varying degrees of Orthodoxy in the Jewish world, there are Orthodox Jews who might be more flexible about shaking hands with a woman. It all depends on each person's personal custom and level of comfort, and in no way are those men who choose not to shake hands with a woman trying to be ill-mannered.

8. Women are not supposed to touch a Torah scroll

One of the very first questions asked of me as a rabbi was whether it was true that a woman is not allowed to touch the holy Torah scroll. Traditionalists argue that a menstruating woman is in a state of ritual uncleanliness and therefore may not touch or hold a Torah lest she transmit her impurity to a sacred object. It is a bubbe meise, however, to think that a woman is not permitted to touch a Torah. Rabbinic law never objected to a woman coming into physical contact with a Torah, even if she were a menstruant. The Talmud is quite clear on this issue when it says that "words of the Torah are not susceptible to uncleanness" (Berachot 22a). This means that a Torah scroll is beyond the possibility of being defiled, since it has such a high degree of holiness. Thus it is permissible for women to carry the Torah, and in many synagogues, including some Orthodox ones, that is the case.

CHAPTER 10

Israel

1. The religion of Israel is more Orthodox than in other parts of the world

Israel has set up a religious system that includes a chief rabbi for Jews who are Ashkenazim and a chief rabbi for Jews who are Sephardim. These chief rabbis align themselves with the Orthodox world, and indeed there are Orthodox Jews in Israel whose allegiance is to these two chief rabbis. The fact of the matter is, though, that a large majority of Israelis are not Orthodox, and thus the individual observance of religious ritual, such as the laws of keeping kosher and strict adherence to the laws of the Sabbath, are no more noticeable in Israel than in any other country.

The holy city of Jerusalem, however, is the exception in this respect. For hundreds of years Jews have flocked to Jerusalem for prayer, study, and meditation. And in Jerusalem there are scores of Orthodox synagogues and religious schools (yeshivot) consisting of adherents whose lives are devoted to a careful observance of the Torah and scrupulous worship at the designated times. Children and adults wearing long black coats and unshaven earlocks are a common sight in the holy city, and on the Sabbath many of the restaurants are closed, and public buses are nowhere to be seen on the streets. In Safed, one of Israel's four holy cities in the north, there are remnants of Jewish mysticism to be found in Orthodox circles. As for the average Israeli in large cities such as Tel Aviv or Haifa, the pattern of Jewish observances varies little from that of other lands.

2. An authentic Zionist believes that all Jews must be prepared to live in Israel

For some Jews Zionism represented the rebirth of the Jewish consciousness. For pious Jews Zionism has meant religious revival. For secular Jews who wanted to preserve the cultural aspects of Judaism, it was a path leading to the goal of Jewish culture. In the early twentieth century those who considered themselves Zionists agreed that it was important for Palestine to be turned into a homeland where Jews would be able to lead an independent national life. Theodor Herzl felt that in time all committed Jews would eventually return to their historic homeland. and the remaining minority over time would eventually disappear through assimilation.

David Ben-Gurion, Israel's first prime minister, posited that a Zionist could only be defined as a person who was prepared to come and live in Israel. And in 1968, in a proclamation issued by the Jerusalem Program of the Zionist Congress, the concept of aliyah, personal immigration, was accepted as the ultimate ideal and requirement of belonging to any authorized Zionist group.

Today, there are many Jews who consider themselves ardent Zionists but have not accepted the call to permanently make aliyah and bring their families to live in Israel. They encourage and support the efforts of other Zionist groups whose goal is encouraging people to live in Israel, but they themselves are not prepared to do so.

3. Zionism is racism

In 1975 the United Nations General Assembly adopted a resolution equating Zionism with racism. This was a terrible slander, and in 1991 it was finally revoked. Zionism is the national liberation movement of the Jewish people, and it holds that Jews, like any other nation, are entitled to a homeland. History has demonstrated the need to ensure Jewish security through a national homeland. Zionism recognizes that Jewishness is defined by shared origin, culture, religion, and history.

Today many Christians support the goals and ideals of Zionism. Israel's open and democratic character and its careful protection of the religious and political rights of Christians and Muslims rebut the charge of exclusivity.

To single out Jewish self-determination for condemnation is itself a form of racism. Civil rights lawyer Alan Dershowitz has written in his book *Chutzpa* that "a world that closed its doors to Jews who sought escape from Hitler's ovens lacks the moral standing to complain about Israel's giving preference to Jews" (p. 241).

4. The Jewish people have no claim to the land they call Israel

A common misperception is that the Jews were forced into the Diaspora by the Romans after the destruction of the Second Temple in Jerusalem in the year 70 C.E., and then, centuries later, suddenly returned to Palestine, demanding their country back. In reality, the Jewish people have maintained ties to their historic homeland for more than 3,700 years, including a national language and a distinct civilization.

The Jewish people base their claim to the Land of Israel on at least four premises: (1) God promised the land to the patriarch Abraham; (2) the Jewish people settled and developed the land; (3) the international community granted political sovereignty in Palestine to the Jewish people; (4) the territory was captured in defensive wars.

Even after the destruction of the Second Temple and the beginning of the exile, Jewish life in Palestine continued and often flourished. By the ninth century, large communities were reestablished in Jerusalem and Tiberius, and in the eleventh century Jewish communities grew in Gaza, Ashkelon, Jaffa, and Caesarea

Israel's international "birth certificate" was validated by the promise of the Bible, uninterrupted Jewish settlement from the time of Joshua onward, the Balfour Declaration of 1917, the League of Nations mandate, the U.N. partition resolution of 1947, Israel's admission to the U.N. in 1949, and the recognition of the State of Israel by most other nations.

5. Israel should not be called a Jewish state

There are Jews (and others too) who are uncomfortable with the view that the United States is a Christian society. For example, Christmas is celebrated as a national holiday with the lighting of the Christmas tree at the White House. By the same token, there are Jews who are reticent about referring to Israel as the Jewish state, since Israel is a democracy and is inhabited by people of a variety of faiths and beliefs.

Where Israel is called a Jewish state, the implication is not that it should become a theocracy, although there is surely a minority that does indeed see it as such. Israel is a Jewish state in that it was founded as a homeland for Jewish people to preserve and promote Jewish values and culture. For instance, the Hebrew language has been revived and is a living language in Israel. Most Israelis are given Hebrew names, and often their family surnames have been retooled to reflect the Hebrew equivalent. Streets have been named after important Jewish people and events in Jewish history. And most significantly, the Law of Return confers automatic citizenship on any Jew who chooses to live in Israel.

With the rapid growth of the Arab population, there are Israelis who posit that if Israel one day loses its majority of Jews, then it can no longer can claim to be a Jewish state. Others hold that Jewish statehood does not depend on population alone, but on historical and cultural considerations and the quality of Jewish life maintained by its Jewish population.

11

Medical Ethics

1. There is one Jewish view on abortion

The Jewish view of abortion is, in some ways, quite simple. If you ask rabbinic authorities to explain the Jewish view on abortion, the answer is almost always the same: "Tell me the case." There is no single Jewish rabbinic view on abortion. There are, however, two extreme viewpoints in the abortion controversy. One says there is no moral justification for abortion, while the other claims it is a woman's right to have an abortion on demand. The debate continues to be a lively and heated one.

Jewish law and tradition have struggled with the question of abortion since Bible times, and even as we move into the twenty-first century the struggle continues. In 1973 the U.S. Supreme Court seemingly decided the abortion issue in the landmark case of *Roe v. Wade*. The court struck down all state laws that prohibited abortion. Yet the debate rages on, and anti-abortion groups continue to push for a constitutional amendment that would prohibit abortion.

The main rabbinic statement regarding abortion occurs in the Talmud (Mishnah Oholot 7:6). The passage reads:

> If a woman is in hard travail [i.e., she finds it very hard to give birth to her child and her life is endangered], her child must be cut up while it is in her womb and brought out limb by limb, since the life of the mother has priority over the life of the child. But if the greater part of it has already emerged from the womb, it may not be touched, since the claim of one life cannot override the claim of another.

The meaning of the Mishnah is clear. It is not permitted to murder one person in order to save the life of another. While the child is still in the womb, it is not a person by Jewish law. To destroy it is to commit an act of murder. Once the greater part of the child has emerged from the womb, it is considered as if the child has been born and the child is then a person in Jewish life. The life of the mother must be saved by destroying the fetus.

Today, rabbinic opinions on abortion abound. Because life is so very sacred, the writings point to a restriction of the legitimacy of abortion to a narrow range of cases. Generally, Jewish law requires abortion when the woman's life or health (physical or mental). is threatened by the pregnancy. Jewish law permits abortion when the risk to the woman's life or health (again, mental or physical). is greater than that of a normal pregnancy but not so great as to constitute a clear and present danger to her.

2. Judaism permits assisted suicide

Jewish tradition teaches that life is a gift from God, and God alone has the right to make decisions about life and death. Therefore, suicide is morally wrong. And since suicide is prohibited, aiding a suicide is also forbidden.

Assisted suicide combines active euthanasia (acting with the intention of taking another's life, but for a benign purpose, such as relieving agonizing and incurable pain) with suicide. In assisted suicide, both the person who wants to die and his or her assistant contribute to executing the death.

Some Jewish ethicists take a more liberal stance on withholding or withdrawing life support systems, including artificial nutrition and hydration, to enable nature to take its course. However, the bottom line is that Jewish law does not permit suicide or assisted suicide.

That being said, it is important to note that Jewish law has always demanded that we take a much more active role in ensuring that the dying are not abandoned to physical pain or social ostracism, and that we make the mitzvah of visiting the sick a critical part of our mission as Jews. Hospice care has also been an important system whereby the patient is supported physically, psychologically, and socially, by a whole team of people, including family and friends.

3. Rabbinic authorities do not permit donation of organs

Although it is forbidden by Jewish law to mutilate a corpse for the purpose of harvesting organs, most rabbinic authorities agree that this prohibition can be set aside in order to save a life. It is in the rabbinic interpretation of saving a life that we get differing opinions.

The greatest consensus of rabbinic opinion holds that eye or corneal transplants are permissible. Transplantation of a healthy kidney to replace a patient's nonfunctioning kidney is also permissible. The general rule is that the rabbis permit organ transplants when they can be accomplished without major risk to the donor's life or health.

The most restrictive rabbinic opinion would permit donations only when there is a specific patient who stands to lose his or her life or an entire physical faculty. According to this opinion, for example, if the patient can see out of one eye, a cornea may not be removed from a dead person to restore vision to the other eye. Only if both eyes are failing, such that the potential recipient would lose all vision and therefore incur serious danger to life and limb, may a transplant be performed. Moreover, according to this more restrictive view, the patient for whom the organ is intended must be known and present. Donation to organ banks is not permitted according to this view.

Each year in November there is a National Donor Sabbath that allows clergy of all religious denominations to speak to their members and try to raise awareness about the critical need for organ and tissue donors. Also discussed are religious beliefs and traditions related to this topic.

4. Brain death is not acceptable in Jewish law

Waiting even a short time is generally too long today, if doctors are able to use a dying person's heart to save the life of an awaiting transplant patient. Consequently a goodly number of rabbis have suggested that a flat electroencephalogram, indicating cessation of spontaneous brain activity, is sufficient to determine death. In 1988 the chief rabbinate of Israel approved heart transplantation, effectively accepting that a flat electroencephalogram guarantees that the patient can no longer independently breathe or produce a heartbeat. This has become the accepted opinion of virtually all modern Jewish authorities, with the exception of some Orthodox rabbis.

5. Using artificial organs or animal organs (including a pig's) for transplants is forbidden by Jewish law

The use of animal or artificial organs is permissible and serves to help two of the major ethical problems regarding transplants. The first is the moral problem of assuring that a vital organ is not removed from a legally living person (so that the transplantation is not an act of murder). The other is the practical problem of providing enough organs for those who need them.

Although questions have been raised about the use of animal parts for direct transplants or for making artificial organs, no Jewish source considers this to be a moral issue. Judaism, after all, does not demand vegetarianism. And if we may eat the flesh of animals under the kosher dietary laws, then we may certainly use animal parts to save a life. Judaism in fact, posits that if the use of animal parts can save a human life, we have a moral and religious obligation to use them, and they do not even have to be derived from a kosher animal.

6. Donating one's body to science for medical student practice is not allowed by Jewish authorities

The answer to this question depends upon which rabbinic authority is asked. There are surely rabbis who would argue that the use of body parts for medical science is both an honor to the deceased and a real mitzvah in that it benefits the living. Of course, one must have the express written permission of the deceased's family.

Objections to the donation of one's body for science center around the desecration of the body and the delay in its burial after death. Many Orthodox rabbis take a very hard line on this issue, claiming that any invasion of the corpse for purposes of a transplant is warranted only if a patient will immediately benefit thereby. Many others do not object to the use of bodies of persons who gave their consent in writing, provided that the dissected parts are carefully preserved so as to be eventually buried with due respect according to Jewish law.

CHAPTER

Prayer

1. For Jewish prayer to be valid, it must be offered in the Hebrew language

Although Hebrew is clearly the preferred language of prayer, Jewish law decrees that we may pray in any language we understand. And if we know how to read Hebrew but do not understand the words, it is always permissible to look at and ponder the English translation, usually found on the opposite page of the prayerbook, in order to understand what we are saying or praying for.

2. Skipping parts of the worship service because you cannot keep up is not permissible

We should take our time and not race through the prayerbook. However, when a prayer service is moving too quickly for a worshiper, it is better (and permissible) to skip parts of the service and say the rest with full concentration than to try to say all of the prayers in a rushed and hurried fashion. Jewish prayer is often called "service of the heart," and heartfelt prayers that are said with feeling are the best kind of prayers and the ones most likely to find their way to God.

The late theologian Abraham Joshua Heschel used to say that to pray is to take hold of a word and stay with it for a while. That was another way of saying "don't rush your prayers."

3. It's untrue that there is a Jewish blessing for everything

B elieve it or not, blessings have been formulated for prac-
tically every experience of daily life—arising from sleep,
dressing, eating, and drinking. There are, as well, blessing for
unusual happenings, such as escaping from danger, recovering from illness, or seeing something wondrous in nature.
There is even a blessing to recite on the death of a loved one
that proclaims God as the True Judge.

The genius of the Jewish blessing formula is the opportunity for the worshiper to establish a close relationship with
God by speaking directly to God. Rabbi Meir, a second-cen-
tury rabbinic teacher, stated that it is the duty of every Jew to
recite one hundred blessings every day. This seems like a lot,
but Jews who recite the three daily services and the other
appropriate blessings throughout their day offer even more
than the required amount.

4. There is no such thing in Judaism as an improper prayer

It's a bubbe meise to think that any prayer one utters is always going to be an acceptable according to rabbinic opinion. In fact, not all prayers were considered proper by the rabbis. For instance, one is not allowed to pray to God for the impossible to occur. Such a prayer is called a "prayer in vain." Here are some rabbinic statement which bear information regarding improper prayers.

We may not pray for an overabundance of good to be removed from us (Talmud, Taanit 22).

Rabbi Judah the Prince said: "It is not permitted to pray for God to send death to the wicked (Zohar Chadash 105).

To pray for the impossible is a disgrace. It is as if a person brought a hundred measures of corn into a shed and prayed: "May it be Your will that they become two hundred" (Tosefta, Berachot 7).

To pray for something that has already happened is a prayer in vain. For instance, if a man's wife is pregnant and he says, "May it be God's will that my wife give birth to a boy," that is a prayer in vain (Talmud, Berachot 54a).

5. Kol Nidre is Yom Kippur's most important prayer

Although Kol Nidre is the most well known part of the Yom Kippur liturgy, in actuality it is not a prayer. Rather, it is a declaration on behalf of the congregation that all vows pertaining to religious obligations that were not fulfilled during the previous year or that may be broken in the year to come shall not be counted as binding.

In ancient times, a person who wished to cancel a vow would appear before a Bet Din, a Jewish court of three persons. On the eve of the Day of Atonement, when Kol Nidre is chanted, the leader of the worship service, often flanked by two persons on either side holding the Torah scrolls, is reminiscent of the ancient Jewish court.

Surprisingly, Kol Nidre was rejected by some very important rabbinic scholars, including Saadia Gaon, because they saw no valid reason to recite this statement of absolution.

In the eleventh century, Rabbi Meir ben Samuel changed the original wording of Kol Nidre to make it apply to vows to be contracted "between this Yom Kippur and the next Yom Kippur." Support for this emendation was provided by a talmudic statement which reads: "Whoever desires that none of his vows made during the year shall be valid, let him declare at the beginning of the year: 'May all the vows which I am likely to make in the future be annulled' " (Talmud, Nedarim 23b). This was in consideration of the frailties of human nature and the tragic results of promises too hastily made and pledges inadvertently undertaken.

6. Judaism doesn't prescribe any particular bedtime prayer

Going to sleep at night can be a scary proposition for some people. Many people have shared stories about the difficulty they have falling asleep. To that end Judaism has a prescribed prayer that is intended to be said by a person in bed before trying to go to sleep. Its intention is to petition God to assist with a night of peacefulness and pleasantness, with fewer bad thoughts that can interrupt a good night's sleep. Following is one of the suggested nighttime prayers:

Praised are You, Adonai, Sovereign of the Universe, who closes my eyes in sleep and my eyelids in slumber. May it be Your desire, God of my ancestors, to grant that I lie down in peace and that I rise up in peace. Let my thoughts not upset me, nor evil dreams. May my family be perfect in Your sight. Grant me light, lest I sleep the sleep of death. Blessed are You, God, whose majesty gives light to the entire world.

Hear O Israel, Adonai is Our God, Adonai is One.

CHAPTER

Bible

1. Moses wrote the first five books of the Bible

The Bible's first five books are known as the Torah and also as the Five Books of Moses. It is true that most traditional Jews believe that Moses was the sole author of these books. But by the time the Talmud was completed in the year 500 C.E, some rabbis were already beginning to question the authorship of certain biblical passages. For example, it is difficult to believe that Moses wrote the description of his own death at the end of the Book of Deuteronomy.

It had long been apparent that different names for God are employed in various biblical passages. In the eighteenth century, a Frenchman by the name of Jean Astruc discovered that when the passages containing each name were separated, two parallel accounts of the same story emerged. His discovery earned him a place in history as the father of the scientific study of the Bible.

Today, most Bible scholars posit that the five books were the product of schools of people who contributed to its writing. Moses, of course, was one of the contributors. The material was gathered and edited over a span of centuries, and that is why we find differing or contradictory statements in the books. Despite all of this, the Torah is a unified work, on the basis of common agreement shared by all its authors about God's important role in the life of the Israelite people.

2. The Bible teaches us that we should never argue with God

When Noah is told by God in the Book of Genesis that the whole world will be destroyed but that he will be saved along with his family and animals, Noah acquiesces to God's command and builds an ark as he was commanded to. At no time does Noah challenge God and God's desire to destroy an entire world. In the next important Bible story, Abraham learns of God's intention to destroy the twin cities of Sodom and Gomorrah, whose reputation for cruelty was well known. Upon hearing of God's intention, the patriarch Abraham tries to change God's mind and asks: Since there undoubtedly are some good people in the cities, how can God destroy the innocent with the wicked: "Shall not the judge of all the earth act with justice?" (Genesis 18:25). Abraham also seems to be arguing on behalf of the evil people. Otherwise, he would have requested that the good people alone be spared. But instead, he appeals to God to save all the people of the cities, provided some good people be found within them.

This first instance of a human being arguing with God became a characteristic feature of the Hebrew Bible, and of Judaism in general. Hundreds of years after Abraham, the psalmist cries out to God in anger: "Awake, why do you sleep, O God. Why do You hide Your face, and forget our suffering and oppression? (Psalms 44:24–25). The willingness to confront God stems from the belief that God, like man, has responsibilities and deserves criticism for failing to fulfill them. Elie Wiesel once said that "The Jew may love God, or he may fight with God, but he may not ignore God."

3. God only speaks to individuals in the Bible, never to the entire people of Israel

It is true that for the most part God speaks to individuals in the Bible (most of them prophets), and they become the spokespersons for the Jewish people. However, in the Book of Exodus, seven weeks after the Israelites leave Egypt, they reach Sinai. There God, for the first and only time, speaks to the entire people, and declares before them the Ten Commandments. The people are terrified by God's dramatic appearance amid thunder and lightning. They entreat Moses, "You speak to us, and we will obey; but let not God speak to us, let we die." Moses assures the Israelites that God has not brought them from Egypt to Sinai in order to kill them. "For God has come only in order that the fear of God may ever be with you, so that you do not go astray" (Exodus 20:16–17). Nonetheless, he agrees that in the future he will relay God's messages to them.

4. The story of Hanukkah is in the Bible

It surprises lots of people that Hanukkah is not mentioned in the Hebrew Bible. Rather, it appears in the books of the Apocrypha, books which are not a part of the Jewish canon. The story of the Maccabean revolt and the rededication of the Temple appears in both the First and Second Books of Maccabees. The First Book of Maccabees was probably written in Hebrew in Judah around 120 B.C.E, forty-five years after the first Hanukkah. The Second Book of Maccabees was written in Greek and was designed to encourage Egyptian Jewry, particularly the large population in Alexandria, to adopt the observance of Hanukkah. In neither story is there a mention of the miracle of the jug of oil that was found in the Temple that burned miraculously for eight days. Rather, in the Second Book of Maccabees the Jews celebrate an eight day festival in which they carry *lulavim* and *etrogim* and chant hymns to God. It appears that Hanukkah began as a second celebration of the eight-day Sukkot holiday.

5. King David wrote the Book of Psalms

M any people hold to the tradition that King David
wrote all 150 of the psalms in the Book of Psalms.
Indeed, fifty-seven psalms begin with the words "Psalm of
David." Most biblical scholars today posit that King David
could not have written all of the psalms. Some of them refer
to historical events that happened hundreds of years after his
death, such as the Babylonian Exile. Others employ words
and grammatical forms that were not in use until long after
David's time. It may be that King David composed a few of
the psalms (the prophet Amos, who lived only a few hundred
years after the time of David, refers to him as a musician and
composer). If he did, surely the famous Twenty-third Psalm
("The Lord is my Shepherd") may have been one of them,
featuring imagery that would have come naturally to David,
the shepherd-warrior-king. It may also be that "Psalm of
David" means "a psalm in the style of David" or in honor of
a later king, a descendant of the House of David.

6. All mitzvot are based on verses in the Torah

Although the so-called 613 commandments all appear in the Torah, there are seven other commandments that the rabbis determined had to be observed that are not based on any verses in the Torah. They have come to be known as rabbinic mitzvot (*mitzvot de'rabbanan*) and include the following:

Washing one's hands before eating
Lighting Sabbath candles
Reciting the Hallel Psalms of Praise
Lighting Hanukkah candles
Reading the scroll of Esther on Purim
Making an *eruv* (a technical term for the rabbinic provision
　　that permits the alleviation of certain Sabbath restrictions).
Saying a blessing before experiencing pleasure in worldly
　　items; for example, before partaking of any food, before
　　smelling a fragrant plant, and so forth.

7. Because there is separation of church and state in the United States, one would not expect the U.S. Constitution and other documents to draw upon the Bible

You may be surprised to learn that even though there is an attempt to separate church and state in the United States, there are numerous American documents that are clearly related to biblical precepts. Following is a listing of several of them along with their biblical counterparts:

> We hold these truths to be self-evident, that all men are created equal, that they are endowed by their Creator with certain inalienable rights, that among these are life, liberty and the pursuit of happiness.
>
> (Declaration of Independence)

> Have we not all one Father? Has not one God created us? Why should we be faithless to each other, profaning the covenant of our ancestors.
>
> (Malachi)

> We, the people of the United States, in order to form a more perfect union, establish justice, insure domestic tranquility, provide for the common defense, promote the general welfare, and secure the blessings of liberty to ourselves and our posterity, do ordain and establish a Constitution for the United States of America.
>
> (U.S. Constitution)

> *Justice*, justice shall you pursue, that you may thrive in the land which the Lord your God gives you.
>
> (Deuteronomy 16:20)

Congress shall make no law respecting an establishment of religion, or prohibiting the free exercise thereof; or abridging the freedom of speech, or of the press; or the right of the people to assemble, and to petition the government for a redress of grievances.

(Bill of Rights)

Proclaim liberty throughout the land, for all of its inhabitants.

(Leviticus 25:10)

8. Knowledge of biblical words cannot improve one's English-language comprehension

On the contrary, a fairly large number of Hebrew Bible words have passed directly into the English language, mostly in a religious context. Knowledge of the Bible can enhance one's knowledge of the meaning of these English words. Here are some of the more well known ones:

Amen. "So be it."

Baal. Name of a Phoenician god, and hence today any idol.

Bedlam, A corruption of Bethlehem, deriving from the notorious insane asylum of St. Mary of Bethlehem. Today, by extension, it means "confusion."

Behemoth. Plural of *behemah* (beast). Perhaps applied to the hippopotamus, but signifying any huge creature.

Camel. From the Hebrew *gamal*.

Cherub: An angelic being, later interpreted to mean a beautiful and innocent child.

Gehenna. Meaning "hell," it derives from the Hebrew *Gei Hinnom* (Valley of Hinnom), a place near ancient Jerusalem where human sacrifice took place.

Halleluyah. "Praise God."

Leviathan. A sea monster or whale.

Manna. Heavenly food, and today any sweet and refreshing substance.

9. The usual depiction of the Ten Commandments in art is a correct one

The pictorial portrayal of the Ten Commandment in art has five of the commandments written on one tablet, and the other five commandments written on a second tablet. When the Ten Commandments are portrayed in art, they are almost always portrayed in this manner. But is this an accurate portrayal?

It is assumed that the two stone tablets were of equal size. All told, there are 172 words in the Ten Commandments. The first five commandments consist of 146 words, and the second five of only 26 words. The second tablet could have been one-fifth the size of the first and still have contained all of the words.

Indeed, all of the commandments could have been written on one single tablet. Archaeologists and Bible scholars now believe that the practice of recording covenants and contracts on tablets was well rooted in biblical times, as was the custom of depositing them in the sanctuary. A 3,500-year-old treaty between a Hittite king and a Mesopotamian king noted that each of the contracting parties had deposited a copy in his respective temple before the shrine of his deity. It has been posited that the Ten Commandments followed the same model: one of the tablets was for the Israelites, and the other was, so to speak, God's copy. Thus, pictorially speaking, if one were to follow this theory, each of the tablets portrayed in art ought to have all ten commandments on it, rather than five on one and five on the other.